I have heard that a person
a person with a theory.
Prophets, speaks to that m⸺. ⸺. ⸺y⸺.⸺ ⸺⸺⸺⸺ ⸺⸺ lessons
of the Ancient Prophets with his own nearly lifetime experience of
counseling and teaching. The results race past theory and land in
the heart of life-experienced truth. The truth of these ancient
lessons framed in a contemporary setting is timeless and
invaluable.
— Dennis D. Frey, ThD
President, Master's International University of Divinity

Using vivid scriptural stories, this book gives us rich portrayals to
help us learn powerful life lessons—and then we can help others
with these in-depth insights. On every page, we are encouraged
that others—even men of old—have experienced similar trials.
Now we can learn how to avoid the potholes of daily life and
follow the good ways of God.
— Virginia Stewart, PhD
HOPE Ministries, Christ Presbyterian Church
Nashville, Tennessee

I absolutely love this book. The writing style is warm and
relatable! I found myself exclaiming "Wow! I didn't know that!"
several times as I read about the ancient prophets covered in each
chapter. I will recommend this book to my friends and my
counselees.
— Julie Ganschow
Biblical Counseling Coalition Council Member
Blogs on counseling issues for women

Howard has done again the very thing he excels at doing, he has communicated the Word of God in technicolor. The Old Testament figures highlighted in *Life Lessons from Ancient Prophets* are so familiar to Howard it is as if he is speaking of old friends and neighbors. The wisdom gained from a fresh look into the Word pierces the heart. This is a worthy read!

— Judy Dabler
 Certified Christian Conciliator
 Creative Conciliation, St. Louis, Missouri

Life Lessons from Ancient Prophets

Howard Eyrich

Life Lessons from Ancient Prophets
© 2018 Howard Eyrich

ISBN-13: 978-1987524932
ISBN-10: 1987524934

All rights reserved. No part of this publication may be reproduced or transmitted in any form or by any means without written permission from the publisher.

Unless otherwise noted, all scriptures are taken from *The Holy Bible, New American Standard Bible®,* copyright © 1960, 1962, 1963, 1968, 1971, 1972, 1973, 1975, 1977, 1995 by the Lockman Foundation.

Scripture marked "ESV" are from *The Holy Bible, English Standard Version®,* copyright © 2001 by Crossway, 2011 Text Edition. Used by permission. All rights reserved.

Scripture marked "KJV" are from *The Holy Bible, Authorized (King James) Version.*

Scripture marked "NIV" are from *The Holy Bible, New International Version®,* copyright © 1973, 1978, 1984, 2011 by Biblical, Inc.™ Used by permission of Zondervan. All rights reserved worldwide. www.zondervan.com.

Scripture marked "NKJV" are from *The Holy Bible, New King James Version®,* copyright © 1982 by Thomas Nelson Publishers, Nashville. Used by permission. All rights reserved.

Published by Growth Advantage Communication
3867 James Hill Circle
Hoover, Alabama 35226
growthadvantage@gmail.com

Dear _____,

I found this book challenging and inspiring.

_____

_____

_____

_____

_____

_____

Given by _____

Dedication

I dedicate this volume to my grandchildren,
and especially to Megan and Claire, my budding writers.

These wonderful children have brought boundless joy to my life. Watching them grow in the Lord practicing some of the lessons cited in this volume in their own lives brings refreshment to my soul. You will be hearing from them from the business sector, to the ministry sector, to the sports sector, to the education sector. They are leaders of their generation.

TABLE OF CONTENTS

INTRODUCTION 11

- LIFE LESSON ONE: What to Do When You Rediscover the Bible for Yourself... 13
- LIFE LESSON TWO: Pray Before You Act 23
- LIFE LESSON THREE: What to Do When There is Nothing Else You Can Do 35
- LIFE LESSON FOUR: Temptation: The Legacy of Yielding 45
- LIFE LESSON FIVE: Sin and Stupidity: Two Sides of the Same Coin 55
- LIFE LESSON SIX: Toying with God Is a High-Stakes Game 67
- LIFE LESSON SEVEN: Grasping the Wonder of Worship 77
- LIFE LESSON EIGHT: Generational Survival Depends Upon the Credibility of Leaders 91
- LIFE LESSON NINE: Five Lessons for Leaders 101
- LIFE LESSON TEN: Displaying the Loving Kindness of God 111

ABOUT THE AUTHOR.. 127
ALSO BY THE AUTHOR 129
SCRIPTURE REFERENCES.. 130

INTRODUCTION

This brief volume is the outgrowth of my personal inductive Bible study. For the past seven or eight years it has been my practice to have an extended personal time with the Lord several days a week (most weeks). Then, after a prayer time, I open a document on my computer and begin to synthesize my notes from the study into a usable document.

At least four quarters of Sunday School lessons have emerged from this process. They were fun lessons to teach because they were very personal. Obviously, they were edited, and frequent visits to good commentaries kept me from promoting error and/or committing *eisegesis*.

Those meditations frequently were exactly what I needed for a counseling situation on the very day they were experienced. As a result, I began sending them to my counseling staff, who also found them apropos for their counseling cases.

You might ask, "How can I use this book?" Good question. Allow me to make several recommendations.

First, read it, enjoy it, and allow the Spirit of God to challenge you.

Second, most likely while reading it you will think, "Oh, Charlie (or Susie) needs to read this!" So, act on that prompting! Purchase a copy and gift it to Charlie or Susie. We have included a lined page, so you can write a very neat personal note of dedication to the recipient.

Third, it is the perfect size for a fall, winter, spring, or even a summer study group.

Fourth, if you have teens or adult children, this book would make a great birthday or graduation gift, or stocking stuffer.

Life Lesson One

WHAT TO DO WHEN YOU REDISCOVER THE BIBLE FOR YOURSELF
Nehemiah 8-10

There are many lessons in the book of Nehemiah applicable to us in the 21st century that have been applicable for the centuries since the book was written. Some eight or ten years ago our church launched into a building program. The theme of that program was "For Coming Generations." The expansion was particularly focused on children and youth and preparing them to periodically rebuild the walls. Our pastor, Dr. Harry Reeder, preached a series from Nehemiah to stir the hearts of the congregation to get involved in building the wall (the necessary buildings) to disciple the coming generations for their challenges. He was not the first pastor to motivate folks from Nehemiah during a building campaign.

If you are a reader of Christian writers addressing the subject of leadership, you have likely encountered Nehemiah in their discussions. For example, Charles Swindoll, encouraging everyday believers to be leaders, lists seven lessons.

- A passion for the project (exemplified by his enthusiasm, drive, determination, and creativity).
- An ability to motivate people (exemplified by his succinct articulation of goals).
- An unswerving confidence in God (exemplified by Nehemiah journaling his prayers).

- A resilience and patience through opposition (exemplified in his dealing with critics).
- A practical balanced grip on reality (exemplified by his directing a "trowel and sword" approach to ensuring safety, as well as posting guards).
- A willingness to be a hard worker and remain unselfish (exemplified by his feeding folks at his own expense).
- A discipline to finish the job (exemplified by focusing on essentials necessary to get the job done and not on perfectionistic details).[1]

We are not going to work through the first five chapters. These are exciting and instructive as we learn why Nehemiah concludes that the good hand of God was upon me (2:18) and we observe the product of that good hand in courage, boldness, leadership, organization, etc.

We will pick up with chapter six which sees the completion of the wall project. Chapter seven records actions to secure the city and *Then my God put it into my heart to assemble the nobles, the officials and the people to be enrolled by genealogies* (7:5) and this leads to organizing the people accordingly. By the seventh month they were settled in their cities (7:73).

There is an interesting and unexpected progression displayed for us in this historical occasion. It is interesting for two reasons. First, the organized dynamics of the project of building

---

[1] http://www.insight.org/resources/article-library/individual/seven-leadership-lessons-that-apply-to-you. Cited 1/26/18. (Although taken directly from Swindoll, I have rearranged elements of his material.)

the wall leads to an interest in the *book of the law of Moses* (8:1). Nehemiah's leadership and the completion of the job under duress inspired the people to want to look more closely at the BOOK. And, secondly, it is interesting because of the progression of the response to the Word. The progression is not what we would expect as we shall observe.

Upon the completion of the wall's construction, Nehemiah and Ezra gather with the people for a town meeting in the square in front of the Water Gate. Ezra stands in a specially constructed pulpit raised above the people (8:5) and reads from the book of the Law of Moses (the Pentateuch). As we read through this passage we discover that not only did Ezra read the Word, but the crowd was organized in groups for Bible study so that what was read was then taught and explored.

If we had the security footage to review, we would see Ezra reading a passage, followed by organizing them into groups, and then instructing the study leaders to lead a discussion as to the meaning and application (8:8) of the passage just read. Then, after probably 20-30 minutes, Ezra would call the group to order and read again, which would be followed by instruction/discussion. This exposure to the Word would lead to deep sorrow and weeping (8:9).

What we have observed on our imaginary security footage leads us now to follow the progression of this wonderful historic record. There are six lessons for us to explore in this account.

First, **do not focus on grieving and regretting the past** (8:9). Yes, when we are freshly convicted upon our return to the Word after neglecting it for some time, we should repent. But, here is an important lesson. Psalm 37:8b says *Do not fret, it leads only to evil doing.* Nehemiah calls them to celebration and instructs them to remember ... *the joy of the LORD is your strength* (8:10) ... *because they understood the words which had been made known to them* (8:12).

When we come to a place of recognizing our sin and reckoning with it through repentance, we must be cautious of our Enemy turning our sorrow into more sorrow (fretting over our past). We need to celebrate the faithfulness of the Lord who brought us to a return to the Word and rejoice in His love and forgiveness.

From time to time I have counselees who suffer from this malady. The PDI (an initial form completed by the counselee providing personal data that gives the counselor a starting point) informs me that this person is depressed. One of the many causes of depression is fretting. The counselee (we eventually dig this out) committed fornication (or some other *gross* sin as a young teenager and this soil upon the conscience, though confessed to God long ago, is a dark cloud through which all else is viewed. One gentleman, in mid-life, fretted so much over his indiscretion as a teen that he refused to use the appropriate medical term when speaking about it. He was a real believer who superficially repented and was locked into regret which, in his case, produced other evil, including the inability to sustain opposite-sex relationships as well as depression.

While we have already mentioned this second lesson, here it is again. **Focus on celebration!** The man born blind said it so well, *One thing I do know. I was blind but now I see* (John 9:25 NIV). We were blind to our sin. The Holy Spirit, using the Word of God, opens our eyes and now we see. Celebrate! A hymn I sang as a teen says it nicely:

> I once was lost in sin, but Jesus took me in,
>
> And then a little light from heaven filled my soul;
>
> It bathed my heart in love and wrote my name above,
>
> And just a little talk with Jesus makes me whole.[2]

The Apostle John put it this way in 1 John 1:7-9 (ESV):

> *But if we walk in the light, as he is in the light, we have fellowship with one another, and the blood of Jesus his Son cleanses us from all sin. If we say we have no sin, we deceive ourselves, and the truth is not in us. If we confess our sins, he is faithful and just to forgive us our sins and to cleanse us from all unrighteousness.*

If I am forgiven, I should be focused on fellowship with Him. I should walk in the Light and not in the darkness of my fret over the past. That is celebration!

---

[2] *Just a Little Talk with Jesus,* Cleavant Derricks, 1932.

The third lesson is this: **Be focused on gaining understanding**. There was an entire day of learning from the Word. Ezra read the Word from that unique pulpit. This was followed with small groups (8:7) with instruction (8:8) that was an intense time with the people standing the duration (8:5 compare 8:7). This was followed by a great festival of celebration at the end of the day (9-12). It is now the second day (8:13). Here is the lesson. When you have been refreshed by returning to the Word, celebrate! And then, return to the Word to ... *gain insight into the words of the law* (8:13).

This was my experience my first summer as a Christian. My mentor and spiritual father made me an offer I could not refuse. He told me if I would go work on the staff of Highland Lake Bible Conference for the summer he would match what they paid me and send it to the university to cover my tuition for the fall semester. I applied, was accepted, and as soon as the school year ended I was off to Highland Lake. Frankly, I had no idea what to expect. I was an eighteen-year-old leaving a solitary home where I grew up as an only child, to go live with eighty-four other teens and college students in dorm-like facilities.

The first week was for staff training as well as conference building and grounds preparation for the season. We arrived on Saturday for what they called "meet and greet." We ended the day with a worship service and preaching. Dr. Bob Ketchman, of General Association of Regular Baptists fame, was the speaker that night and throughout the week. On Sunday Dr. Bob spoke for morning and evening church with small group discussions following each service. Dr. Bob spoke every morning the entire week at 9:00 and every evening at 7:00. This was followed with a small group meeting to discuss the teaching of the hour.

During my first year as a Christian my Bible exposure was limited to Sunday morning church and Wednesday night teenage club. This first week at Highland Lake was a lot like what the people experienced with Nehemiah and Ezra. I found myself anxiously awaiting the next teaching time by Dr. Bob. I understood the Word, what he was teaching, and desired to *gain insight into the words of the law* (8:13). The people discovered what they had not been doing and set out to be obedient (8:14-18). I discovered what the Lord was doing in my life and at the end of the week, along with 82 of the 85 staff, committed my life to the Lord for whatever He desired.

The fourth lesson is in chapter nine verses one through three. It is this: **Do focus on repentance.**

Their initial response to the Word was, I think, regret that they had neglected the Law of Moses. Now, after implementing a return to the Word by celebrating the Feast of Booths, during which the Word was read regularly (8:18), they came to more fully grasp their sin. This did not lead to regret, but to genuine repentance (9:1-3). This repentance took the form of corporate reading for four hours and corporate confession for four hours.

The remainder of chapter nine records the essence of their confession by remembering their history of arrogant failures and prayers of thanksgiving for God's faithfulness. This is the fifth lesson: **Do focus upon thanksgiving** for God's good hand upon you (2:18). About a month into that summer at Highland Lake, I was involved in a serious accident that could have resulted in blindness and ruined lungs. God saw fit to protect me from a life-altering injury. The month of intense teaching by a gifted teacher prepared me to walk through this contingency with a solid handle on the grace of God. The accident, coupled with the teaching, fostered an attitude of thanksgiving in my young Christian heart. It prepared me for the next step of life, my first semester at Bob Jones University.

The final lesson that I want to draw from this story is: **Do focus on renewing your commitment** (9:38-10:39). This is a common lesson found many times in the ancient prophets. Here is what these people under Nehemiah's leadership concluded. *Now because of all this we are making an agreement in writing; and on the sealed document are the names of our leaders, our Levities and our priests"* (9:38). It is good to make written agreements before God and to make covenants with God before witnesses. Whether people realize it or not, this is what they do when taking biblically-framed vows in their marriage ceremony.

For example, when Jock Polinski,[3] a 50+ year old immigrant with a Roman Catholic background, became aware of what he had done when he married his wife, he was thoroughly rattled. He was a line worker in an auto assembly plant. He and his

---

[3] Not his real name.

wife came to our counseling center in a Presbyterian church (given their age and religious background, I was really surprised to see them). His wife was crushed by his complete lack of loving her as Christ loved the church. About the fifth session, I walked them through the fact that they had made a covenant with God to fulfill their vows to each other. I walked them through what that looks like biblically. Toward the end of the session this tough, hard man looked at his wife and said, "I guess I am going to need to change the way I treat you. If this is what I said to God, then I need to change." After all these years, I am sure those were not his exact words, but they capture the essence of what he said. And he did change. He heard the Word of God explained and he responded with repentance.

On that last night of the staff training week at Highland Lake, we did not make a written agreement. But we did stand and walk to the front and kneel before the pulpit. Dr. Bob was our witness. It was a solemn night, and for me, it was as good as a written agreement. There have been many times along the way when I needed to repent for drifting. However, the agreement before God that night some sixty years ago has been my mooring. From time to time the Holy Spirit has grabbed me and shaken me, which has led to repentance and renewed affection for the Word and fellowship with Jesus—a good example of Nehemiah 9:27-31.

If you continue to read the history of Israel—as encapsulated by Ezra's prayer in Nehemiah 9—it becomes very evident that this, with all its sensual experience (touch, work, engagement, public repentance, etc.), did not secure the nation. Every generation must have its wall building, its re-engagement with the Word, its repentance, its agreement with God. Every generation is responsible to communicate the faith to the next generation (Deuteronomy 6:1-10), but each generation must receive it, embrace it, and practice it. So may you, my reader, be motivated by this account to re-engage with the Word of God so that it will convict you and refresh your heart and mind. Re-engagement calls for hearing the Word, studying the Word, and then implementing the Word.

Life Lesson One

True repentance leads to celebration and renewed interest in exploring the Word.

Personal/Counseling/Mentoring Applications

1. Do a personal inventory. How vital is your engagement with the Word of God?
2. Set aside a day for an intense Bible study with a trusted friend to include four hours of study and four hours of interpersonal interaction, helping each other to evaluate the quality of your walk with Jesus.
3. Mark your calendar for a once-a-month slot of one hour to do nothing but celebrate God's good hand upon you and your family.

Life Lesson Two

PRAY BEFORE YOU ACT
AND
RECOVERING WHEN YOU FORGET TO DO SO
1 Chronicles 17

I have one of those minds that runs in overdrive most of the time. When people ask my wife, "What will he do when he retires?" she replies, "He will never retire or run out of projects even if he lives three lifetimes." Unfortunately, there are many times that an excellent idea has popped into my head, and I have run with it only to see it smashed against the wall of reality. Other times I find myself mildly depressed because I have a great idea but know I cannot make it work, either for lack of funds or time. I end up grieving the idea, resulting in a mild depression.

Since having bypass surgery, I have been more deliberate about planning time and activities with my son and the rest of my family. I grew up on a farm in Pennsylvania. Most farm boys in the eastern part of the state learned to hunt rabbit and pheasant. I was no exception. Since college, between my work life and our living locations, there has been little opportunity to go pheasant hunting. Bud, a man I discipled some thirty years ago is an avid hunter. One day I picked up the phone and re-established contact with him and inquired as to whether he still made trips to Kansas to go pheasant hunting. We determined that on New Year's Day he, my son, and I would get together to begin planning a hunt for next fall. The next morning I was praying over the New Year and the events that were already on the schedule. When this anticipated meeting came to mind, I found myself praying about the hunt.

"Lord, I would like to hunt with my son and Bud. It would make a great memory and a special time for my son to cherish over the years. If possible, I'd like to do this. And, Lord, while we are planning it, guide our choices so they coincide appropriately with the weather patterns to make it a successful trip. And, Lord, if this is not something for which we need to be spending time and money, help us to recognize it and accept it."

How different this process was from many other times an idea has surfaced. Rather than just organizing the men to join me, gathering the information, and whipping out a credit card to make the deposit, I prayed first.

Twenty years ago, I joined the staff of Briarwood Presbyterian Church under the leadership of Rev. Frank M. Barker.[4] I knew Frank casually as a fellow minister in the Presbyterian Church in America. I knew something about the uniqueness of Briarwood. But, at fifty-seven, I did not anticipate the spiritual impact on me that flowed from my relationship with Frank. That was probably the result of my not having been close to Frank. The greatest influence Frank had in my life was through his attitude of prayerfulness. Frequently, as I walked the halls of the church, I would see Frank with his hand on someone's shoulder, praying. In my staff responsibility, I met with Frank once a week. When I

---

[4] For an inspiring read get a copy of *Flight Plan,* written by Janie Buck and published by Christian Focus, which is the biography of Frank Barker. It is an uplifting and spiritually stimulating read.

walked into his office he would greet me, small talk for a few minutes and then just breaking into a sentence, he would say, "Let's pray." He'd bow his head and offer up a very simple conversational prayer over the subject matter of our meeting. On many occasions, I sat in meetings with a difficult agenda and in the middle of a tense moment Frank would just chime in and say, "Let's pray" and just start praying. There was no pretense, no fanfare, and no emotional display. He would just start talking with the Lord as a member of the committee and ask for His intervention, wisdom, guidance, and calming hand upon our human emotions.

So, you see, Frank influenced my view of and practice of prayer. I began to understand Paul's injunction, *Pray without ceasing* (1 Thessalonians 5:17) with a fresh perspective.

Well, what does all this have to do with the theme of this book, Life Lessons from Ancient Prophets? That is a good question, so let me answer it. Suppose you invest $10,000 in a new up-and-coming tech stock, and five years later you wake up one day to find that the company has exploded, and you have become a multi-millionaire with great prospects of reaching 100 million dollars in the next two to three years. Suppose also that you were one of the founding members of a church plant that had struggled to break the 100 mark in regular attendance, and was still meeting in a school building for worship, and its offices located in a local strip mall. After you recover from the shock of your "good fortune" you turn to your wife and say, "I'm going to call the

Pastor and tell him I am going to build that first building for the church. I can give the church 2.5 million dollars now and another 2.5 million dollars next year." She replies, "Oh! That would be wonderful! Please, call him right away."

What is missing in this scene? You guessed it! Prayer! But, you protest, you did not need to pray about something like this. It is obvious that they need the building. It is obvious that you have the money. It is obvious that their meeting situation has hampered the ministry. It is obvious that God would be pleased with this action. You could easily conclude that God had placed them in this church plant and directed this investment for such a time as this. So, why should you pray?

There was a time that I would have agreed. I planted a church 40 plus years ago. We were in temporary quarters, a township building, and then a firehouse for five years. Our congregation would grow to about 100-125 and then regress back to 80-90. One couple told me, "We love the preaching/teaching, but you have no program for our teens and no place for them to meet." They were the tenth family who said something similar. I told this couple, "If all the families who have voiced similar concerns had stayed, we'd have 15 or 20 teens now and likely the funds to acquire property upon which to build." If you were in my church and you called me to say God had prospered you beyond belief this week and you wanted to give 2.5 million dollars to the church to build our first building, I would have said, "OK, meet me at the Downingtown First National Bank at 10:00 this morning and we'll transfer the funds." I would not have said, "Let's pray about that and see if God says 'Yes.'"

Well, this is a modern version of what we read in this Old Testament narrative. In 1 Chronicles 15, King David finishes building a house for himself and pitches a tent for the Ark of God. We then find a narrative recording the movement of the Ark of God to Jerusalem to occupy this tent. Chapter 16 narrates the wonderful worship service that King David organizes to celebrate the movement of the Ark to Jerusalem. Then in chapter 17 verse 1 the narrative continues with King David having a stroke of humility and generosity at the same time. To paraphrase, David says to himself, "Here I am living in this luxurious house and God is out there dwelling in a tent. It ought not to be so. I am going to build God a house." So, he calls his trusted friend and prophet, Nathan, and announces his idea and asks what Nathan thinks. Verse two gives us Nathan's response. We may paraphrase it as, "Great idea, David! Go for it!"

That night the Lord comes to Nathan and says, "Bad idea, Nathan! I have a message for King David. Go tell him, *"You shall not build a house for Me to dwell in!"* (1 Chronicles 17:4) Wow, how would you, if you are the wife of a newly minted millionaire, like God to shake you awake in the middle of the night and say, "Go tell your husband that I don't want him to give 2.5 million dollars to build a church building! I have another plan."

Not only does God tell Nathan to order David not to proceed, but He instructed him to remind David that He was in control. Here is what God says to David through the prophet:

- I called you.
- I made you.
- I have been with you.
- I have cut off your enemies.
- I will honor you.
- I will take care of My people.
- I will build the house of David.
- I will establish your son and his kingdom.

So, God says to David, "I have a plan and you building me a house is not in that plan. That will be your son's task."

What is the lesson for living that we learn from this Old Testament narrative? It is this: no matter how God-honoring our plan or desire may be, we need to seek God's will and direction before proceeding. Does this mean that our ideas and creativity should be scuttled? No, it means we should submit them to God in prayer. It means that we should be living life *praying without ceasing* so that our attitude is one of submission to Him—always!

David's response to God's overruling his idea is also instructive for us. In verses 16-27 the narrative records David's prayerful response to God. In this prayer, we find a wonderful model for our response to God when He overrules our great ideas. There are at least five components to this response. They are:

- Humility (v 16)

- Thanksgiving (v 17-20)
- Submission (v 21-22)
- Concurrence (v 23)
- Worship (v 24-27)

Well, I don't know about you, but this narrative strikes close to home for me. It also has been one that I have accessed with frequency as a pastor and counselor to encourage people to pray "before they jump" and to help them recover when God stops their great ideas.

One of my invited reader critics responded:

> "It is in the everyday decisions that I need more help. Maybe you could expound on some of the simple, everyday issues that come our way in which we forget to pray. And, for me, it would be the words that come out of my mouth without thought, much less prayer, that often get me into trouble."

So, to my friend and to my reader I would say the following. Before you go to bed at night, take a few minutes to list those items on your agenda for the next day. Begin each day with a few minutes of concentrated prayer. First petition God as your Father (*Our Father which art in heaven ....* Matthew 6:9 KJV). Second, tell Him that you desire to honor His Name in all you do today and to contribute positively to His Kingdom coming a bit more into reality through your life. Specifically seek the wisdom from your Father for each situation that will come your way today. Then take your list and pray through each item asking God to lead you in the issues as they ensue.

Third, if you have a particular problem, like the words that pop out of your mouth, each day ask the Lord to enable you to guard your thoughts and your tongue. Perhaps it would be helpful to put James 1:19 on a 3x5 card and place it in a conspicuous place to remind you to guard your mouth. Your choice here is to decide to make preparation to overcome your weakness.

Such simple steps can lead to great gains. But, since they are so simple, people most often decide not to implement them. The result is continued failure, guilt, and dealing with the pain of the circumstances that are generated. Biblical decision-making is not always about big life-changing events like whom I should marry. Tending to godly biblical decision-making principles in the smaller everyday issues builds these into one's mind-set so that when the data-faith integration point of a decision comes upon us, we have acquired the skills for competent decision-making, the main one of which is praying.

Praying is bowing our soul before the Lord. I sometimes ask people to tell me who the Lord is. They usually look at me with a quizzical expression. I coach them until they begin to name at least five non-communicable attributes (attributes that are uniquely God's). Then I say, now remember, when you pray He is your Father who works on your behalf through all these awesome character traits.

Prayer leads us to thanksgiving. Draw a line with an arrow on each end. Let one direction represent the past and list at least three times when you have prayed and seen the Lord very distinctly answer your prayers. Now thank Him for those answers. Turn your attention to the other direction of the arrow and let that represent the present. Thank God that you can trust Him to hear and answer prayer regarding your current concerns.

As you pray and give thanks, ask the Lord to enable you to submit to His will in the matter of your concern. If His answer is no or wait, ask Him to enable you to submit to His wisdom and plan.

The step of thanksgiving will prepare your heart to concur with His plan. It is a wonderful experience when you scrap your clever idea to concur with God's plan and suddenly see just how unique His plan turns out to be.

The foregoing four steps are living worship. But, engaging in this process leads you to a very conscious decision to worship. What that worship looks like will be dependent upon your personality and your cultural experience.

A friend went out to plant a church in a very nice suburban southern city.[5] He did not need to leave his previous thriving church. Denominational leadership had prayerfully sought the right man to be the point man to not only plant this church, but to become the leader who would spawn an expanding church planting process in that city. The pastor prayed when he was contacted and

---

[5] This is a true story. I have chosen to keep it generic to protect the privacy of those involved.

asked to consider this possibility. A select group of pastors within the denomination were asked to pray about urging their churches to pledge a significant gift toward funding this project.

When the project was launched there were many clever ideas prayed over and jettisoned as the Lord worked through those involved to realize the good ideas that were good, but not the right ideas for that time and place. The Lord had another idea—His idea.

They were meeting in a temporary building that did not fit well in the cultural context. One Sunday a woman who had visited on several occasions came to the pastor after the service and shared that her divorce was final that week. Her husband had been unfaithful multiple times and divorce was her chosen response. She was very sad, as evidenced by the tears rolling down her cheeks. The pastor listened, offered some words of comfort and then asked if he could contact her ex-husband. "Sure! But, I doubt he will listen to you; he has not listened to anyone else."

The pastor made an appointment and met him for lunch. At the lunch the pastor walked him through the gospel and asked, "Is there any reason why you should not receive this freely offered gift of eternal life?" He answered, "No" and prayed with the pastor. Several months later, after counseling and discipleship, the pastor re-married them. The husband, who was well known in the business community, invited his high-level business friends to the wedding. At the wedding the pastor presented the gospel and instructed the couple and the congregation in the biblical view of marriage. Over a period of several months four or five other men sought out the pastor with similar responses, "I never heard a wedding ceremony like that. Could we meet?" He was used of the Lord to lead each of them to Christ. In the Providence of God, these men became both the spiritual and financial leadership of that church. This was God's idea.

It was man's idea to plant this specific church. It was an idea spawned by God in The Great Commission. There were many times along the way that ideas were prayed over and buried. There were many times of sadness or depression when ideas hit the wall of financial constraints or disappointment in the lack of people following through. Each time the pastor and those God drew around him recovered as they continued to prayerfully press onward.

As David gained God's guidance, he pressed on to facilitate Solomon's completion of the dream. We do well to pray, to listen, to adjust, and to press onward trusting that God will guide.

LIFE LESSON TWO

No matter how God-honoring my plan or desire may be, I need to seek God's will and direction before proceeding.

PERSONAL/COUNSELING/MENTORING APPLICATIONS

1. List three times when you have had a good idea, proceeded without consulting the Lord, and saw the Lord bring the idea to naught.
2. Take each one of these incidents and ask yourself:

a. From what did God protect me?
   b. In retrospect, why was my good idea not the right idea for the situation?
3. Remember a good idea that God did not let you carry out but let someone else carry out. If you have not already observed how this person was more suited to execute the good idea, prayerfully ponder the question, "How was this person better equipped to execute this good idea?"

Life Lesson Three

WHAT TO DO WHEN THERE IS NOTHING ELSE YOU CAN DO

1 Samuel 1:1-2:11

I have always enjoyed human interest stories. The people in difficult circumstances who have struggled with the determination to overcome have been my heroes. Abraham Lincoln was one of my childhood heroes. My mother had a children's book from which she read to me on many occasions. My favorite story was the one about the life of Lincoln.[6]

Now it happens that I was born on Lincoln's birthday. When I was maybe three or four, Mom read his story to me on my birthday. When she finished, I looked up at her and said, "Mom, I don't want to become president because I don't want to get shot." His determination enabled him to achieve greatness, but it put him in harm's way. I was inspired by his achievement of greatness and sorrowed by the price he paid for that achievement.

I have always enjoyed watching people. During my college years if I did not have a date for the Artist Series (we had eight of these formal events each year), I would go early and sit in the balcony to observe fellow students. Watching them fascinated me. Their choice of clothing for an event, the way they related to one another, their response to the event, and their personal peculiarities

---

[6] If you have not read about all the failures Abraham Lincoln experienced and all the obstacles he overcame, take a few minutes to access this site and you will be amazed and awed.
http://www.abrahamlincolnonline.org/lincoln/education/failures.htm

often occupied more of my attention than did the performance. For example, on one occasion I watched a very attractive young lady who obviously had burned the midnight oil one too many nights. She was desperately fighting to stay awake, but old man Sandman was victorious. Her head dropped sharply. When it did, her hat, which was gently perched upon well-groomed hair, went tumbling, bouncing off the person in front of her, and went plummeting over the balcony railing into the audience below. It was a most amusing event! Particularly because this event was the formal church service in the university auditorium and Dr. Bob Jones Sr., founder of the university, was preaching.

In 1 Samuel 1 we have one of those stories that should inspire us to godly greatness. It is the story of Hannah. In every society and historical period Christians have found themselves hard pressed by the impact of sin in the world. Though Hannah was an Israelite, living in a theocratic (God was the King) society, she found herself part of a multi-wife household. It is clear from Genesis 2:23-25 that God intended marriage to be a union of one man and one woman. But early on man developed polygamy.

Shakespeare observed, "What tangled webs we weave." In this brief story of Hannah, we get a glimpse of the tangled web of polygamy. Hannah's husband, Elkanah, loved her. She was the wife that he enjoyed. If you think of the story in modern terms, she is the wife he took to a five-star hotel for a getaway weekend. She drove the Mercedes convertible. She slept in the master bedroom and had the jetted tub bathroom. Her rival, Peninnah, was the object of Elkanah's provision and care. Scripture says, *When the day came that Elkanah sacrificed, he would give portions to Peninnah his wife and to all her sons and daughters* (1:4 ESV). Again, to think in modern terms, she drove the Dodge van. Her children's clothing came from Sears. Her boutique was Walmart. She shared a bathroom with her children in the other wing of the house.

But Peninnah had something that Hannah desperately desired. She had children. Hannah had a closed womb. Peninnah liked to "rub it in." Peninnah, the writer of Samuel tells us, *would provoke her bitterly to irritate her, because the LORD had closed her womb"* (1:6).

One of the details of this story is instructive for us. It was on the occasion of Elkanah preparing his family, in their home town in the hill country of Ephraim, to travel to Shiloh to sacrifice that this rivalry sharpened. Watching various groups of believers over the years has revealed that this is a common pattern. Whether it is a youth group going to camp for a week of spiritual development, an adult mission trip, or even a group of preachers assembling for a time of study, prayer, and planning, the tensions in the group intensify. While the occasion for the tensions, a rivalry between two wives, is certainly different, the observable behavior is very similar. There is taunting, provoking, and irritating one-upmanship resulting in hurt feelings, tears, and frustrations.

Some years ago, I had a counseling case in which a woman was estranged from her sister. Her sister was married to a blue-collar worker, lived in a modest part of the city and drove a van that had seen better days. But her sister had three lovely children and this lady had none. My counselee was depressed and not a pleasant mate. Her husband was exasperated. His wife had been a cheerleader in college. She was a vibrant participant in life with him for the first five years of marriage. She terminated her career path to relieve the stress in her life so that she could become pregnant. It had now been three years since the doctors told her that she would not be able to conceive. While the details are different, the husband's response was the same. Elkanah was frustrated and said to Hannah, *Why do you weep and why do you not eat and why is your heart sad? Am I not better to you than ten sons?* (1:8). My counselee said to his wife, "Why are you so stuck on having a child? Do I not love you and care for you and provide everything you desire?"

Men have not come very far in three thousand years! Elkanah was insensitive and my counselee was insensitive. Elkanah and my counselee were focused upon the practical. The deep emotional struggles of their spouses were not on their radar screens.

These struggles and strong emotions over years intensified with the birth of each child. Peninnah's incessant taunting during this journey brought Hannah to the place that she asked herself, "What do I do when there is nothing else I can do?" Her answer is seen in verse ten. *And she, greatly distressed, prayed to the Lord and wept bitterly* (1:10). Most certainly we are not to conclude that she did not pray about this matter regularly. But we, like Hannah, do not pray many times with the intensity (distress and deep frustration) observed here in the temple. However, there are times when the Lord allows us to be stretched by great frustrations in order that He can prepare us to pray with absolute abandonment, full and passionate intensity, and a readiness for complete submission.

Listen, this is what we hear in Hannah's prayer. *She was deeply distressed and prayed to the LORD and wept bitterly.* And she vowed a vow and said:

> *O Lord of hosts, if you will indeed look on the affliction of your servant and remember me and not forget your servant, but will give to your servant a son, then I will give him to the Lord all the days of his life, and no razor shall touch his head* (1 Samuel 1:10-11 ESV).

First, note that her prayer reveals that she was at the end of her rope in attempting to understand her predicament. Her reasoning process had hit the wall. She was deeply distressed. Probably the best understanding of the Hebrew word would be "frustrated." She had exhausted every rational explanation. She examined her heart and did not find anything in her life that should account for the fact that she could not have a child. Second, observe that she was emotionally intense; she wept bitterly. Being rationally and emotionally distraught, she prayed with such intensity that Eli suspected her to be drunk and proved to be a rather unthinking and insensitive pastor. His rebuke did not deter Hannah. She offered a reasonable defense when she replied, *No, my lord, I am a woman troubled in spirit. I have drunk neither wine nor strong drink, but I have been pouring out my soul before the* LORD. *Do not regard your servant as a worthless woman, for all along I have been speaking out of my great anxiety and vexation* (1:14 ESV). To his credit, Eli listens and offers comfort by speaking as God's official, ... *the God of Israel grant your petition ....* (1:17 ESV).

My mind goes to a parable of the importunate widow told by Jesus (Luke 18:1-8). Hannah was not a widow, so obviously, Jesus did not have her in view when He spoke this parable, but we are certainly reminded of the parable when we read about this incident in her life. The main lesson of Jesus' parable is clearly that we ought to pray, we ought to pray intensely, and we ought not give up until God answers our prayer. There are three characters in this one-act play that Jesus creates in this story—the insistent woman, the insensitive and unjust judge, and the infinite Judge, divine and righteous.

The lesson of His parable is this. **Prayer requires perseverance and patience.** As with the widow, so with us, it may seem that God's ear is shut. The asking is in the present active indicative, so the implication is that we are to be continuous in our praying, and, as with the widow and Hannah, ratcheting up our intensity. The Judge is not like the judge who does not hear. He hears, but sometimes His delay has the purpose of our preparation. This seems to be the case with Hannah. Her waiting and the emotional intensity prepare her to recognize that the gift of her son is special and therefore she is prepared to give him to the Lord.

So, what do we do when there is nothing else we can do? The same thing we should be doing all along—going to the Lord in prayer. However, as with Hannah, so with us, the Lord sometimes allows us to come to the end of ourselves, a conscious awareness that we have exhausted all options. In so doing He prepares us to come to Him very consciously. And sometimes He allows this flow in our lives because He has something special He desires to do in us and/or through us, and He must prepare us both to receive it and give Him all the glory for it.

This is exactly what we see in the life of Hannah: God's plan to give Samuel to Israel through Hannah. Allowing the taunting to lead her to the rational and emotional brink prepared her to be utterly submissive to the Lord and to be desperate enough to be willing to give her son back to the Lord for His purposes. While it is not likely that any of us are going to play such a significant role in God's Kingdom, that which He desires to do through us is of no less importance to Him. We should be living lives in which prayer is an integral daily part, but there are times in which God allows the circumstances of life to bring us to the brink of exhaustion. At those times we should pray with such intensity that an observer may mistake us for being drunk. And, we should pray with the assurance that the God of Israel will grant our petition, realizing and accepting that it may not be as we have planned it. Like Hannah, that answer may not work out exactly as we anticipated. I doubt that Hannah understood, when she took Samuel at about age five to live with Eli, that her son was never coming home. I am reasonably sure she saw this as a dedication and educational experience and that her son would return home to grow up at the hand of her tutelage. After all, is that not what Peninnah had and what she envied?

However, Hannah was prepared for God's purpose because in her prayer she rested her heart in the hands of God. In the same manner we need to rest our hearts in the hands of God.

Life Lesson Three

When there is nothing else you can do, go to the Lord in prayer.

Personal/Counseling/Mentoring Applications

1. Determine and write down something that you think is within the will of God (you can pray about it in Jesus' Name) that you have prayed about, but God has not answered. Discuss this matter with a trusted godly friend and enlist that friend to pray—with you and for you so that you will persevere till God answers—yes, no, or wait.
2. Consider reading/studying one of these:
    - *How to Pray When You Don't Know What to Say,* Elmer L. Towns, Regal Publishing, 2006

- *Lord, Teach Me to Pray in 28 Days*, Kay Arthur, Harvest House Publishers, 2008
- *How to Pray*, R. A. Torrey, CruGuru, 2008.
- *How to Pray: Reflections and Essays*, C. S. Lewis, HarperOne Publishers, 2018

3. Consider watching this video series by R. C. Sproul: https://www.ligonier.org/learn/series/prayer/how-to-pray/

It is thus very true that we shall find consolation only through the scriptures, which in the days of evil call us to the contemplation of our blessings, either present or to come.

~ Martin Luther ~
Luther's Works, Vol. 42, p 124

Life Lesson Four

TEMPTATION: THE LEGACY OF YIELDING
2 Samuel 11
(Numbers 20, Exodus 17)

The two most disappointing narratives in the Old Testament (other than the fall of Adam and Eve) are this one concerning David and Joab, and the account of Moses striking the rock (Numbers 20). There is a significant similarity. Both men chose disobedience. And both men lost an incredible opportunity. Moses was directly disobedient.

If you read the passage you will note that unlike the first time the people were complaining of being thirsty, when God told Moses to strike the rock and begin a stream of fresh water (Exodus 17), on this occasion God specifically instructed him to speak to the rock. Instead of following the instruction, we read:

> *Then Moses and Aaron gathered the assembly together before the rock, and he said to them, "Hear now, ye rebels: shall we bring water for you out of this rock?" And Moses lifted up his hand and struck the rock with his staff twice, and water came out abundantly, and the congregation drank ....* (Numbers 20:10-11 ESV).

The Lord's response immediately follows the incident. Here is what the Lord says to Moses:

> *And the Lord said to Moses and Aaron, "Because you **did not believe in me**, to uphold me as holy in*

*the eyes of the people of Israel, therefore **you shall not bring this assembly** into the land that I have given them* (Numbers 20:8-12 ESV, emphasis added).

Then, as the people were poised to enter the Promised Land, God informed Moses that this sin of disobedience had closed the door to his entering the land (Numbers 27:14).

In the passage before us in 2 Samuel, David is not in his place of responsibility. The writer tells us that *In the spring, at the time when kings go off to war, David sent Joab out with the king's men and the whole Israelite army. They destroyed the Ammonites and besieged Rabbah. But David remained in Jerusalem* (11:1 NIV). Moses did not do what he was told to do, and David did not do what he was expected to do. In making this choice, David put himself in position to be tempted.

Commentators and preachers have a field day with David's choice. Some have suggested that he had seen Bathsheba on previous occasions and planned this whole scenario. After all, he was in the position to do so. He was commander-in-chief. Some have suggested that David was innocent of evil intent. Bathsheba, they suggest, was the one with evil intent. She positioned herself to catch David's eye. They see her as the woman of Proverbs 5.

The simplicity of the text is this. David put himself in position to be tempted by not exercising his responsibility to lead his men (11:1-2).

The first lesson that we learn from the narrative is this: do not avoid responsibility and put yourself in a position where you can be tempted.[7] In all the accounts of David's warfare, he is leading his men. Even years later, as an older man, while fleeing the rebellion of Absalom he is involved in leading his men.

The second lesson to be learned from the narrative is this: when temptation occurs, flee (11:3)! Timothy was a young pastor who was a timid man working in a sexually charged city. The Apostle Paul tells him, *Flee also youthful lust* (2 Timothy 2:22 KJV). David had multiple opportunities to flee. When he looked and saw Bathsheba, he could have said, "Whoa! Lord, help! This is wrong!" He had to send a man to bring Bathsheba to him. That took a conscious decision. He had a moment to shut down the temptation. When he took her in his arms, that took a conscious choice, and feeling the warmth of her body was surely a red-light warning to flee. And third, at the initiation of sexual contact there was that last fleeting moment to cry out, "No, Lord, I can't do this; help me run!" But, having intentionally run through the blinking

---

[7] Back in the mid-1970s my associate was counseling a man who suffered from regular self-satisfaction. This man was serious about changing as demonstrated by the fact that he flew several hundred miles every other week to come to counseling. After four or five sessions, my associate questioned the man as to the time of day when his issue occurred. His reply was a bit odd for he indicated that it was immediately after arriving home from work. Upon further investigation it was revealed that he walked to and from work about six city blocks and that he passed through the X-rated movie theater district. The reporting of this practice was introduced by the statement, "I walk home and take the shortest distance between two points." My associate replied, "You are no longer taking the shortest way home for you have been exposing yourself to temptation by gazing upon all the marques. Obviously, there were other issues, however, limiting his exposure to this temptation was significant in his growing victory.

yellow warning lights of his conscience, he made the choice to send someone to get her. This was his moment to resist and terminate the temptation. So, while he could have fled at any point, not fleeing at the initial point virtually locked him into running the red light and following through on the temptation.

But there is a reason David gave into the temptation, a very human reason. He, though operating within the legalities of the cultural framework, had taken multiple women into his harem. In so doing, he conditioned himself to satisfy his desires.

There is an important lesson to be learned here. We need to make it a practice to not indulge our sensuality. Temptation comes from many quarters. Yes, sexual indulgence is highly contagious and easily habit-forming as those who have tasted pornography have sadly learned. The fact of the matter is gluttony, materialism, narcissism, and a host of other sins can become so engrained that the temptation to indulge is intense and giving in to temptation difficult to resist.

The bottom line regarding temptation is this. DO NOT ACT on it! *One evening David got up from his bed and walked around on the roof of the palace. From the roof he saw a woman bathing* (11:2 NIV). At this point David acted on the temptation. The things I have written up till now are accurate, but the reality is that once the initial taste is experienced you are on a slippery slope. David quickly went from seeing her, to observing her beauty, to inquiring about her identity, to sending for her even when he found out she was Uriah's wife.

More than one young person in the counseling office has confided how they went from hearing about the effects of a certain drug, to researching it on the internet, to mentally speculating about the excitement of a drug trip, to seeking out their first hit. The best course of action is to STOP at the first link. Flee! Each link indulged makes stopping the slide down the slope more difficult. A simple non-sin illustration may be helpful.

My hobby and relaxation is building a model railroad in both HO and N gauge. Because I buy materials online from various vendors many promotions populate my mailbox. I have learned that unless there is something I have planned to add to the collection or use it on a particular project, to not open sales promotional materials. To do so is to be *tempted* to purchase a deal that is too good to pass over. So, I've learned to flee the temptation, hit the delete button and immediately move on to responding to other email that needs attention.

David did the dastardly deed. The text does not accuse him of rape and perhaps that is too strong a word. But I am not sure what word to use when the man who holds supreme autocratic power tells a woman he wishes to sleep with her. So, whatever you wish to call it, David did it. She returned home. Probably within six weeks she sent a message to the King informing him she was pregnant. Immediately David conceived a plan to right a wrong with another wrong. In fact, he tried to right two wrongs. First, he attempted to trick Uriah into sleeping with his wife by calling him back from the front lines for a meeting. Uriah was a man of such integrity that he would not satisfy his sexual desires while his men were on the front lines.

Such integrity pushed David to the point of being desperate. If you are a reader of novels, you have encountered this dynamic before. George had access to the company safe. Though no one knew, he found the combination while searching for a file on Henry's desk one afternoon. He knew Henry kept a hoard of cash in that safe and he knew that Henry's nephew, who hated George, was the only family member with the combination to the safe. One night he was overcome with the temptation to help himself to the stash. He executed the pilfering enterprise skillfully, with one exception. A button from his blazer which carried the insignia of his family crest on its face caught in the door and was torn free from his sleeve. He did not have time to search for it before he knew the night watchman would make his rounds.

Several days later he was in the nephew's office and saw the button on his desk. Earlier that day the nephew had made a remark about blackmail to George. Immediately upon seeing the button he understood the remark and realized the nephew knew he was the thief. He determined he would have to kill the nephew to preserve his secret. He planned a wrong to cover his wrong.

King David takes the process to another level. He decides to cover the wrong with a right (11:27). He marries Bathsheba. A frequent exhortation from the Bully Pulpit of old Dr. Bob Jones, Sr., Founder of Bob Jones University, was this: "It is never right to do wrong in order to get a chance to do right." From King David we learn another lesson: "It is never right to do right in order to cover a wrong."

On the horizontal plane these strategies sometimes work. People get away with crime by covering crime with another crime or even with right action. But such strategies never work vertically. Our omniscient God sees all, knows all, and executes justice. David records in Psalms 32 and 38 the personal agony of his guilt and pictures God, as it were, turning down the screws on him. In Psalm 51 he records his repentance after he is confronted by Nathan the prophet with those awesome words—*Thou art the man* (12:7 KJV)!

Let me summarize for you the lessons in this narrative.

First, **do not position yourself for temptation** (11:1-2). The deacon who takes the collection plates from the sanctuary to the business office alone positions himself for temptation. The pastor who meets with a female congregant at his office without another woman present in the immediate area is both positioning himself for temptation and for accusation of improper conduct by the woman.

Second, **immediately flee temptation** (11:3). Some 30 years ago I had a female counselee. My thirteen-year-old daughter was working the front desk just outside my door. After the counselee departed, it occurred to me that she had very stealthily placed a temptation before me. I told my daughter about it (first step in immediately fleeing). When the woman returned for the next session, I began with a kind but firm confrontation.

"Mary (not her real name), I had the distinct impression at our last session that you were offering a very nuanced invitation to an improper relationship. If I am wrong, please tell me. If I am right, admit to the sin and decide if you desire help with your issues. If you desire help, I am willing to work with you. Otherwise, it would be best to excuse yourself and leave." Mary sat quietly for what seemed an eternity and then said, "You are right. Please forgive me. I do want help." This was the second step in fleeing temptation for me. It was also Mary's first step to a changed life.

Third, **do not act on temptation** (11:4). King David acted upon the temptation. Think of the opportunities he had to not do so. He could have turned, and immediately spoken with his Father. Remember his Psalms? He had a very conversational relationship with God. He generally practiced dwelling or abiding in fellowship with the Father. He had to call a servant to send for Bathsheba. This was another opportunity to not act on the temptation since it took thought and action to give the orders to the servant. When Bathsheba arrived, he had opportunity again to have second thoughts, call in servants and have them gather the wives of the other generals and throw a party to celebrate their husbands' service to the kingdom.

You get the idea. In almost any temptation, there are opportunities to NOT act on them.

Fourth, **do not attempt to fix a wrong with another wrong** (11:6, 15). We have already dwelt on this point, but it bears another look. How often in modern American politics do we observe this tactic! Someone has been unmasked over some temptation to which they have fallen. The next action in the political playbook is to deny wrongdoing. This is often followed by an elaborate scheme of lies. If you are a member of the over-the-hill gang, you will remember Watergate and the fact that it led to the deposing of Richard Nixon and jail sentences for the henchmen who executed the temptation to spy to win. Things have not changed in the 21st century as the machinations of the last election so graphically testify.

Fifth, **do not cover a wrong with a right** (27). Tolstoy, in *A Confession*, reminds us that "Wrong does not cease to be wrong because the majority share in it."[8] Somewhere along the way I read or heard that Patrick Henry said, "The eternal difference between right and wrong does not fluctuate; it is immutable."

The United States Marine Corps says, "Do the right thing, in the right way, for the right reasons."

The Bible says, *Whatever your hand finds to do, do it heartily as unto the Lord* (Colossians 3:23; Ecclesiastes 9:10 NIV). You cannot cover a wrong with a right in the Name of the Lord who is holy—it is absolutely incongruous!

These action steps (lessons) will provide the opportunity to deflect the temptation, engage with God and others in a positive manner, and assure that you will not build a legacy of yielding to temptation. These action steps could have enabled King David to

---

[8] https://www.pinterest.com/explore/leo-tolstoy/

leave a very different legacy. God forgave him. God continued to use him. God graciously recorded his failure and the legacy of yielding to temptation for our instruction. Let us learn and avoid the legacy of yielding to temptation.

Life Lesson Four

Fleeing temptation is the best remedy for temptation!

Personal/Counseling/Mentoring Applications

Personal: Do a self-appraisal and identify responsibilities you tend to avoid. Next, ask yourself where your mind tends to wander when you avoid these responsibilities. For example, you choose to not attend a Wednesday night activity at your church. When you do, what do you do instead or upon what do you let your mind dwell?

Counseling/Mentoring: Have your disciple or counselee identify the last three times he/she has sinned.

1. For each sin identified, encourage this individual to pinpoint the occasion for the temptation to which he/she responded.
2. Now encourage him/her to develop a contingency plan for each sin identified to deflect the next temptation. Determine an action which not only diverts attention but replaces the occasion for the temptation with an occasion to give thanks and engage in serving another person.

Life Lesson Five

SIN AND STUPIDITY: TWO SIDES OF THE SAME COIN
2 Chronicles 17

Over the years of working and ministering there have been numerous times when I have thought, "My, why did this individual make such a stupid choice?" On other occasions my private response to someone's self-reported behavior has been, "This is so obviously sin, so how could you as a Christian make this choice?" Or, "It must have been obvious that making this choice was going to end badly, so what motivated it?" If you are like me, there have been at least a few times when you have looked in the mirror and asked yourself one of those questions. The story of Jehoshaphat highlights these questions and helps us see that sin and stupidity are opposite sides of the same coin and how easily a godly person, even just humanly speaking, a good person, can slip into spending this coin.

This seventeenth chapter of Second Chronicles begins by summarizing the earlier life of Jehoshaphat. This summary begins with the assertion of his God-given opportunity to be king and lays out his platform for success. That platform had two major points. On the horizontal plane it was organization and protection (17:2) and on the vertical plane he hearkened back to the glory days of David (*he followed the example of his father David's earlier days* 17:3). There were two dimensions to this vertical platform that remind me of what the Apostle Paul wrote to the Thessalonians, *how you turned to God from idols* (1 Thessalonians 1:9). Somebody I read something like this: Jehoshaphat did not seek the Baals (idols) but sought the God of his father. Let me put all this in practical terms. On the positive side, Jehoshaphat was obedient. He followed the commandments of God. On the negative side, he did not imitate the sinful ways of Israel (the northern kingdom of divided Israel). To put it yet another way, he **chose** to do right, and he **chose** to not do wrong.

This platform for his life and reign over Judah produced very practical godly results. First, we read that God established His kingdom. For Jehoshaphat this meant that he had political and social control that benefited his subjects. They responded positively and enriched him (*he had great riches and honor* 17:5).

Second, we are told that he was energized in the service of the Lord.[9] *And he invested great energy or zeal in the ways of the Lord and again removed the high places and the Asherim from Judah* (17:6).

In other words, as king, he took a personal interest in the religious life of the country by investing energy, time, and finances

---

[9] If you are reading the NASB this is one of those rare times when these translators made a poor choice. While the Hebrew גָּבַהּ can be translated pride the context obviously begs for another option. The word is much more accurately translated contextually as great zeal or eagerness regarding his service of the Lord. גָּבַהּ LN 25.68-25.79 (qal) be devoted, formally, exalt, i.e., have a state of zeal and eagerness, with an implication of giving oneself to a behavior, as an extension of assigning high status to an object and so placing high value to it (2 Chronicles 17:6+) [verb, qal, active, prefixed (imperfect) sequential, singular, masculine, third person]. Swanson, James: Dictionary of Biblical Languages With Semantic Domains: Hebrew (Old Testament). electronic ed. Oak Harbor: Logos Research Systems, Inc., 1997 [emphasis mine].

in the growth and development of the people. He did what good leaders do. He led by example.

Third, he engaged in intentional evangelism and discipleship (17:7-9). He took the initiative to appoint and organize officials. The officers of the civil courts were appointed to teach the people how to appropriately live in the kingdom. The priests were organized and charged to teach the book of the law of the Lord in order to instruct the people how to appropriately worship God and develop a godly worldview.

Fourth, his obedience created an environment of respect that produced political safety (17:10-11).

The fifth practical result was that his obedient leadership influenced the development of leadership in his nation (17:12-19). Godly and good leadership inspires leadership. Godly and good leaders don't gather a leadership team; they develop a team of leaders.[10] He developed a team of leaders.

Wow! Don't you wish your next pastor, CEO, or President of the United States would follow this example? I am sure you are saying, "Yes!" Well let's move into chapter eighteen and follow the story and see how sin and stupidity shows up in this great man of God.

Our first glimpse is in chapter eighteen and verse one: *Now Jehoshaphat had great riches and honor; and he allied himself by marriage with Ahab.*

---

[10] Dr. Harry Reeder turned this phrase and repeated it frequently in the Leadership Team Meetings at Briarwood Presbyterian church during his tenure as Senior Pastor.

Now the name Ahab may not ring a bell with you, but the name Jezebel certainly will. She was Ahab's ruthless, wicked, scheming, arrogant wife who upon her death was eaten by the dogs (1 Kings 21-22). Ahab was a selfish, navel-focused individual who engaged in idol worship and by example led his nation into gross disobedience to God. Surely, we must ask the question, why would Jehoshaphat marry into this family? The answer is actually very simple. Civil war between Israel and Judah had become common since the days of Jeroboam and Rehoboam. One of the chief ways of securing your nation from the attack of a neighboring nation in ancient times was to form an alliance by marriage. Jehoshaphat married the daughter of Ahab to form an alliance and it worked. We do not read of any civil war during his reign. But there is a price to pay for such alliances. There is an obligation to be an ally in the time of war.

We learn (18:2) that after some years, Jehoshaphat went to visit Ahab. It is likely that Ahab called for this conference to enlist him in his desire to go to war with Ramoth-gilead. What plays out is an amusing but sorrowful story. Ahab lays out his plans and asks Jehoshaphat if he will join him. Jehoshaphat understands the alliance he has made by marrying Ahab's daughter and replies "I am your ally, my people as your people, so, 'yes,' I go to war with you. But before we jump into this fire fight, could we seek a word from the Lord?" (My paraphrase of 18:3-4). Ahab agrees and sends for his prophets, his "yes-men".

We are not told why he calls in four hundred when the history of biblical prophets is a chorus of one (Nathan to David, Daniel to Nebuchadnezzar, Moses to Pharaoh). Perhaps there is some irony here in that later four hundred and fifty prophets serving Ahab are challenged by Elijah and destroyed (1 Kings 18:18-46). Nonetheless, he calls in his four hundred prophets and they give a thumbs-up in unison. Jehoshaphat is not convinced. Remember, he has been living obediently for years. He has heard the Word of the Lord being taught. He has been observing the results in his own nation. He is very uncomfortable with this alliance and is probably regretting his brilliant plan to marry the daughter of Ahab to secure his nation from civil war. So he asks, "Is there not one prophet in your nation who speaks for the Lord? Don't you have at least one conservative[11] prophet in this nation?"

Ahab answers, "Yes, there is Micaiah! But, he never has anything good to say to me. You would think I was pagan or something, the way he talks to me. I hate him!" Jehoshaphat responds, *Let not the king say so* (18:7)! This is probably as much an expression of his fear of the Lord as it is a rebuke to Ahab.

Ahab brings in Micaiah. Now the story really becomes amusing. There are two scenes running in parallel. In one scene we see the officer of the court going to fetch Micaiah and coaching him to join the other prophets with a thumbs-up. In the other scene is this side show of the four hundred prophets attempting to gain

---

[11] Obviously, this is a contemporary term. Ahab represents liberal practical atheism. Jehoshaphat desires to inquire of a prophet who adheres to traditional theology.

attention for themselves (18:10) and at the same time validating themselves with a unanimous chorus of "Go for it! God will give you the victory."

Micaiah plays with Ahab. He gives him what he wants to hear, thumbs-up (18:14). But Ahab knows Micaiah. He has been to this circus before (18:15) and tells him, "Give it to me straight! What is the truth from the Lord?" We should not view Ahab's words as genuine. He has drifted so far off course that he views God with no more dignity than the pagan gods he worships.

Micaiah not only gives a prophecy of defeat, but reports a heavenly scene that unmasks the four hundred deceiving and deceived prophets (18:21). For his reward Micaiah gets a slap on the face by Chenaanah the leading false prophet and is consigned to lock-up to be served only bread and water (18:27). Micaiah then gives Chenaanah a personal prophecy of disgrace (18:23-24).

Now we see stupidity as the opposite side of sin. The marriage alliance years before was sin. It was depending upon the worldly philosophy of security through marriage alliances. Marry a man's daughter and he is not likely to attack your nation. Often we see Israel and Judah adopting the world's philosophy to secure their position. Sometimes God directly rebukes such action as in 2 Chronicles 16:7, for example, and other times we just see the fallout as time passes.

If you just heard a dependable prophet of God tell you that you were going to be defeated if you went to war, would you go? If you just heard that God had allowed a deceiving spirit to infiltrate these other four hundred prophets who were saying "you will win," would you go to war? If you knew that you were going to lose a war would you agree to dress in your commander-in-chief uniform while your counterpart dressed down to the uniform of a private (17:29)? Sin led Jehoshaphat into an alliance that obligated him, or at least this was his perception. Sin led him to be stupid.

How often in life do we form such an alliance, or at least perceive it to be so, where we have obligated ourselves in some fashion and act stupidly as a result? Think of the pastor who responds to a female parishioner in the alliance of confidentiality and then discovers that she has had an affair with another member of his church and they have embezzled funds from the offerings to pay for their interludes. His well-intentioned sin of giving unconditional confidentiality has now placed him in the position to act stupidly. He feels wrongly obligated to his vow to secrecy, but he knows that this matter must be exposed to protect the purity of the church and the integrity of the families involved.

There is an honorable way for him to recover, just as there was an honorable way for Jehoshaphat to recover. Jehoshaphat could have said to Ahab, "I owe you allegiance, for I am committed to be your ally, but I owe God a greater allegiance. I cannot join you in this war. I cannot join you even if it means you will turn against me in a civil war." However, as we observe in this story, stupidity is the more likely response.

This pastor could say to this woman, "I sinned when I promised you blanket confidentiality. My intent was to build an alliance of confidence with you so that you would be honest and allow me to help you. However, the sin that you have confessed is not something that can be resolved without the breaking of my promise to you. I would still rather not break your confidence, so I want you to listen carefully to what the Word of God says about dealing with your sin. You do have my full promise to stand with you and walk you through this demanding situation you have created. Please forgive me for my sin against you in making a promise I cannot keep because it violates God's directive." Unfortunately, all too often this will not be the action of the pastor. He will stupidly try to cover his tracks by trying to help cover her tracks.[12] Just think of some of the political scenarios we read in the newspapers these days.

Perhaps we can recognize this dynamic quickly by thinking of a child. Any of us who are parents will remember the time we caught our child in a lie that was crafted to protect a sibling. We were sure that the child was aware that we knew he lied. But his alliance with his brother (the kinship of brotherhood) overrode everything else and he stood there flat-footedly lying to defend his brother. He knew that "a prophet" had informed us of the truth. He knew he was going to lose (be disciplined), but he lied anyway (acted stupidly).

Can we recover from such stupidity? Yes, Jehoshaphat did. When he returned home from the lost battle, the prophet Jehu

---

[12] I have used a very extreme illustration to drive home how stupidity evolves from sin, even well-intentioned sin of a blanket pledge of confidentiality in hopes of helping another escape the full consequence of an action.

greeted him with these words. *Should you help the wicked and love those who hate the LORD and so bring wrath on yourself from the LORD? But there is some good in you, for you have removed the Asheroth (idols) from the land and you have set your heart to seek God* (19:2-3). What follows this rebuke is a renewed commitment to live a godly life personally and professionally. Unfortunately, however, we see that Jehoshaphat had a weakness for alliances with wicked folks.[13] Even after years of walking uprightly again and seeing the Lord provide a miraculous delivery of the nation against great odds (20:1-30), he resorted to making an alliance with the wicked (20:35-37).

There is another lesson we can learn from Jehoshaphat. It is this: beware of character weaknesses. Though you may overcome them sometimes, beware! You will have a penchant for this sin and the stupidity that follows. Little wonder the Word of God tells, *Therefore let him who thinks he stands take heed lest he fall* (1 Corinthians 10:12 KJV)![14]

Where has Jehoshaphat shown up in your life? What can you do to guard against following his example? How can you depend upon the Lord and avoid situations in which you are tempted to

---

[13] This factor in Jehoshaphat's life reminds us to be alert to cultural patterns that we have absorbed. A boy who has grown up in an environment in which lying to escape dealing with a difficult situation is practiced will have a penchant to follow the practice unless he teaches himself to be very wary in difficult circumstances.

[14] A concordance study, using the King James Version, revealed that the warning "take heed to yourself (yourselves)" occurs 61 times and the injunction, "take heed" 57 times. Scanning these one hundred and eighteen verses you will find that many of them deal with on the idea of being careful about recurring sin.

spend this two-sided coin of sin and stupidity? Your Achilles heel may not be anxiety, but the lesson is the same. Plan not to fall! Consciously depend upon the Lord to enable you not to fall. Keep your focus on doing right! Trust your loving and sovereign Lord in everything.

LIFE LESSON FIVE

It is wise to be wary of ungodly cultural norms less you fall prey to sinful stupidity.

PERSONAL/COUNSELING/MENTORING APPLICATIONS

Personal: Pray and ask God to help you honestly review your life and identify where you have been a Jehoshaphat. Don't be embarrassed. We have all sinned and we have all been stupid.
1. Evaluate these incidents and look for a common thread that motivated you.
2. Then, prayerfully devise a plan for yourself that will enable you not to make that mistake again.

Counseling/Mentoring: Ask the counselee/mentoree to do these things:
1. Pray and ask God to help you honestly review your life and identify where you have been a Jehoshaphat.
2. Evaluate these incidents and look for a common thread that motivated you.

3. Prayerfully devise a concrete plan for yourself that will enable you not to make that mistake again and devise an alternative pathway.

The first address of the temtper to Eve was designed to awaken distrust in the goodness of God and doubt as to the truth of the prohibition: "Hath God said, Ye shall not eat of every tree of the garden?" ... The next was a direct assault upon her faith. "Ye shall not surely die" but, on the contrary, become as God Himself in knowledge. To this temptation she yielded, and Adam joined in the transgression. From this account it appears that doubt, unbelief, and pride were the factors which led to this fatal act of disobedience.

~ Charles Hodges ~
Systematic Theology (abridged version)
Edward N. Gross, Editor, p. 273

Life Lesson Six

TOYING WITH GOD IS A HIGH-STAKES GAME
1 Samuel 4, 5, and 6

When the average American—Christian or not—reads 1 Samuel 5:1-5, she is struck with the foolishness of pagan religion. However, if she backs up to chapter 4 verses 1-5 she will discover that those who profess faith in the God of Israel (the self-revealed God), can be as superstitious as pagans.

Let's consider first the foolishness of the Israelites. To do so, we must catch the flow of the history and we must recall the nature of the Ark of the Covenant. The prophet Samuel was the answer to the prayer of his barren mother Hannah, the beloved wife of Elkanah (1 Samuel 1-2). Out of a grateful heart for answering her prayer and granting her a son, she dedicated Samuel to the Lord (1:27-28). She brought him as a boy to live with and be mentored by the high priest, Eli.

Eli had two sons who were in line to follow their father as priests of Israel. However, they were highly immoral young men whom their father spoiled rotten. The result of Eli's failure to properly raise them (2:12) and exercise adult professional discipline when they despised the offerings of the Lord (2:17-25) and practiced immorality with the female servants of the tabernacle (2:22), was that he and his sons were put under the judgment of God (2:32-35). The boy, Samuel, begins his priestly and prophetic career by delivering the confirmation of God's message of judgment to his mentor (3:15-18). News of Samuel's prophetic ministry spread quickly because the Lord *let none of his words fail*, i.e., prophecies fail to come true (3:19). All of Israel from one end of the country (Dan) to the other end (Beersheba) knew that Samuel was confirmed as a prophet of the Lord (3:20). His adult "coronation" as a prophet occurred at Shiloh where God revealed Himself to Samuel by His Word (3:21) and *Thus the word of Samuel came to all Israel* (4:1). Hence there was no excuse for the political leaders not to seek the mind of the Lord through Samuel.

However, God used man's arrogance and self-will to bring about the judgment that He had already determined to execute upon Eli, his sons, and disobedient Israel (2:32-34). The arrogance and self-will of these leaders is embedded in chapter four verse one. Our forefathers, who put the chapter divisions into the Bible, demonstrated their grasp of the dynamics of the account by beginning chapter four with the phrase, *Thus the word of Samuel came to all Israel* rather than using this phrase to end chapter three. In so dividing the chapters, they clearly and rightly imply that though the leaders of Israel were fully aware of Samuel's access to the Lord, they leaned rather on their own emotional reactions to the amassing of the Philistines on their border. They decided to engage in the battle without inquiring of the Lord for direction. Such failure led to defeat!

Frequently Christians who follow the path of these Israelites come to the office seeking counsel. They know the Lord, or at least profess to know the Lord, yet, they abandon the means of grace.[15] They have not been faithful in seeking the Word of the Lord. They have not been faithful in corporate worship. They have not been connected to a small group of believers who could have helped them monitor their slide into an arrogant manner of life in which they were making decisions without seeking the wisdom of God. The failure to seek the Lord resulted in failure on the battlefield for Israel. It is the same way in the life of the Christian sitting in the counseling office; the "Philistines" have won the battle and their lives are in disarray.

Like the Israelites, Christians ask the right question. *Why has the Lord defeated us today* (4:3)? All too often the Christians, like the Israelites, don't seek the Lord for the answer to this question. Like the Israelites, in arrogance they decide what action to take. The Israelites turned their religious symbol—the Ark of the Covenant—into a superstitious tool to manipulate God.

---

[15] Two days after I wrote this paragraph a young woman told me her story. She was reared in a good church. She grew up in a whole family. She became a Christian as an early teen and was very active in the church. She graduated from a major university in our area. She was hired by a major company and quickly became the second highest sales producer in her department. To her surprise and extreme disappointment, she was laid off. She became angry at God. Her reasoning ran like this: "If God loved me why did He allow this to happen to me? I did not deserve it. If He could not control it, then why bother with Him?" She dropped out of church. She moved out of her parents' home and disassociated herself from her Christian family. Now three years later she found herself suffering an "anxiety disorder," financial collapse, and on the edge of being unemployed as a consequence of the downturn in the mortgage business. As the conversation developed, it became apparent that out of her arrogance and self-will, a bitterness toward God and her abandoning of the means of grace ("I packed my Bible in a box and that is where it has been since.") flowed a stream of sin that complicated her life. Like the Israelites, she suffered defeat at the hands of the *Philistines* when she failed to seek the Word of the Lord.

Christians turn prayer into a tool to manipulate God. On the Personal Data Inventory form completed by all counselees that come to our office, there are four open-ended questions to answer. One of those questions asks, "What have you done about your problem?" The most frequent one-word answer is "prayed." When I investigate the nature of the praying, I find that it has been a post-problem bargaining with God to extricate themselves from the consequences of their self-directed decisions.

Like the Israelites, Christians can generate a lot of religious fanfare and thereby gain much attention (4:4-11). Turn on your TV on a Sunday morning and go channel surfing. You will find a lot of fanfare. You will find a prosperity gospel. You will find an invitation to be healed by touching the TV set while the preacher prays over you, along with a million others. You will find invitations to attend meetings at your city auditorium where you are promised to be blessed. You will be asked to give seed gifts to your host who, with some research, you will discover lives in a multi-million-dollar estate. If you are attentive you will see him arrive at the auditorium in a fleet of luxury automobiles accompanied by a security squad.

Religious fanfare gains a lot of attention both from other Christians and the world system. We saw this illustrated in 2007-2008. A number of these high profile religious organizations and individuals with their borderline, at best, religious business practices stirred much discussion in the halls of congress generating a reaction much like that of the Philistines in chapter four verse eight. As a result, they have generated an animosity that has flowered into congressional investigations. In turn, through their foolishness, all Christian organizations have come under scrutiny.[16]

Rather than seeking God through His Word, in the traditional setting through the Prophet Samuel, Israel sought to use God in a manipulative manner to achieve their own ends (in this case, security). Too often, the church today, rather than seeking God through His Word, tries to use God to secure its own ends, too. I observed this in one city where I lived. Over a period of twenty years, two churches suffered demise. Both died for the same reason: Immigrants were transforming their communities. These churches (and individual Christians within them), rather than turning to the Word of God to hear God's voice in their situation, used God as a shield to attempt to ensure their security and continued existence as the church they had been, rather than embracing the immigrants and transforming these local churches into local churches congruent with the new community. They suffered defeat and died.

In the chapters that we are considering, we have revealed for us the decreed will of God. Eli's sons were going to die, Eli

---

[16] Lillian Kwon. *Grassley Concludes Senate Probe of 'Prosperity' Televangelists*. The Christian Post. Jan. 7, 2011. A Senate investigation into the spending of six televangelists concluded Thursday with a list of concerns and a call for the formation of a federal advisory committee to ensure religious organizations comply with laws. Three years after launching the probe, Sen. Charles Grassley, ranking member of the Committee on Finance, released a staff review of the practices of the popular media-based ministries.
https://www.christianpost.com/news/grassley-concludes-senate-probe-of-prosperity-televangelists-48383/ Cited 7/11/2017

was going to die, and with their deaths his family's appointment to the priestly office was going to cease. The prophet Samuel would take up this priestly role. Similarly, God has told us what He is doing behind the scenes to accomplish His purposes. God is still at work accomplishing His decreed will. He has provided us with a broad stroke picture of that which will come through prophecy. In our individual lives we do not know the specifics of the decreed will of God. However, we do know that He has decreed and thereby predestined us as believers to be *conformed to the image of His son* (Romans 8:29) and that at the appearing of Jesus this will be fully accomplished (1 John 3:2).

What have we learned from the example of the Israelites? It is this: there is a high cost to toying with God. God is Holy. What does that mean? It means at least this: that all of God's attributes work in perfect harmony and simultaneously. I don't understand how this reality, perfect justice and perfect mercy, functions at the same time, ("His ways are not my ways" Isaiah 55:8-9). But we can see from this passage and many others that God who is loving is also righteous and just. His attribute of love is fleshed out in interplay between His righteousness and His justice. One neither negates nor ignores the other. We worship the God of Abraham, Isaac, and Jacob, who is the God of Israel (and the God and Father of Jesus Christ). What we see pictured in these Old Testament narratives should be instructive to us. We should expect God to be consistent with His character today as He was then.

We should not be surprised that the pagan representatives of the world system would toy with God as we see pictured in chapter five. I always read this chapter with amusement. The Philistines' first action makes sense. They captured the Ark of the Covenant and they took it to their house of religion and set it beside the idol representative of their god, Dagon. There were many idols of Dagon. The Philistines apparently viewed this place as the central domain of Dagon. Putting the Ark of the Covenant beside him likely symbolized for them Dagon's domination over the God of Israel (4:8) who was represented by the Ark.

The amusing dimensions of the story begin the next morning. A priest of Dagon comes to the temple to perform his religious service and discovers an interesting phenomenon. *Dagon has fallen on his face to the ground before the ark of the Lord* (5:3). In other words, Dagon is in a worshipful prone position before God! What does the priest do? He gets help and they set Dagon upright. Ah, good! Dagon is back in control with the God of Israel beside him. Well, not for long. Can't you imagine this priest? He has a restless night. Then just as the first light of day is breaking he hears a loud thump. He grabs his robe and runs to the temple, where he finds Dagon in a deplorable condition. This time he has not fallen into a prone position of worship, but rather that of a defeated warrior who has been dismembered. About that time reports begin to pour into the priests from all over the city of Ashdod of great physical suffering from tumors (5:7).

The amusement continues. The Philistine lords convene a high command conference and make a brilliant and strategic decision: to bring the Ark of the Covenant around to the city of Gath. Now I may be wrong, but it occurs to me that there was a lot of rivalry among these Philistine lords so that the lord of Gath seized an opportunity to gain an advantage among his peers. I can hear him say, "Gentlemen, bring that religious shrine to Gath. We will secure it!" I suspect the residents of Ashdod were more than happy to concur with his solution. Scripture provides a record of the outcome of this brilliant move (5:9). Next, we find the lords of the Philistines sending the Ark to Ekron. Again, the scriptures do not give us much detail, but I suspect that Ekron was the weakest city of this Philistine confederation. The residents conclude that *"They have brought the ark of the God of Israel around to us, to kill us and our people"* (5:10).

While they may have been the weakest city of this federation, they were the savviest. They appeal to the lords, *Send away the ark of the God of Israel, and let it return to its own place, that it may not kill us and our people* (5:11). Since God had clearly manifested Himself on the very first day of His arrival in the Philistine territory (5:3), it is amazing, to the point of amusement, how men toyed with God. It is clearly seen in the fact that it took them seven months to call a conference to figure out how to send the Ark home (6:1-2).

A plan is conceived, and the Ark is returned to Israel (6:4-18). At this point in the story, God reminds us once again that believers cannot toy with God without consequences any more than the world can. God had established the parameters for handling the Ark (Numbers 4:15). The men of Beth Shemesh allowed their curiosity to drive their response to the Ark rather than God's Word. As a result, God disciplined these men thereby reminding Israel that He was God, alive and well (6:19).[17]

How do you and I handle the Word of God? Do you and I attempt to "use" God? Do you and I seek God regularly through His Word and prayer so that when decision time[18] comes our first response is to pray for wisdom and begin to think through the Word of God to determine the mind of God? Let us be careful that we do not toy with God.

LIFE LESSON SIX

The example of the Israelites teaches us that there is a high cost to toying with God. God is Holy.

PERSONAL/COUNSELING/MENTORING APPLICATIONS

1. What would you tell a young Christian man who says he does not have the resources to tithe?

---

[17] http://www.innvista.com/culture/religion/bible/compare/beth.htm
This reference provides a good discussion regarding the number of Israelites that were struck down. In the final analysis it is dangerous for God's people to toy with him whether it was 70, 570 or 50,070 who were struck down.
[18] See my booklet, *Decision Making and the Will of God* published through Kindle, for an in-depth discussion of the relationship between the will of God and the responsibility for making decisions.

2. What would you advise a college student who seldom spends time studying the Bible because he must invest all his available time studying for courses?
3. How could you use this passage to challenge a young woman who writes her parents every Friday to keep them happy because they are paying for her graduate school?

Life Lesson Seven

GRASPING THE WONDER OF WORSHIP
1 Chronicles 15-16

I grew up with a mother who suffered great loss. She bore six children prior to me. She lost all of them with the most devastating loss being the accidental death of my sister, Betty, at age eight. My mother attended church as early as she could remember. Unfortunately, it was a liberal German Reformed church where the gospel lived only in the liturgy.

My father was not a Christian, although he did not oppose church attendance or Bible reading. My memories of church started at about age seven when we moved to the farm in Brecknock Township, near Reading, Pennsylvania. Our church was rural. We shared the building with a Lutheran congregation. On alternate Sundays, the German Reformed pastor and the Lutheran pastor led services. The services were ritualistic, and the sermons[19] were boring. Obviously, my understanding and appreciation of worship was nil.

There was a religious bright spot, however. From the fourth grade through the eighth grade the Good News Ladies, representatives of Child Evangelism Fellowship, showed up at our school on Friday afternoons at about two o'clock. They taught

---

[19] Years later after my conversion this pastor picked me up one day while I was hitch-hiking. By this point I could recognize theological liberalism. In his conversation this pastor exhibited liberalism which explained the boring sermons of my youth under his tutelage.

Bible stories using a flannelgraph board and led us in singing gospel choruses. Providentially, this made up for my lack of Sunday School experience.[20]

At the age of seventeen the Lord orchestrated my life to prepare my heart to hear the gospel. That hearing occurred at a youth banquet organized by a teenage club led by a businessman and his wife. These activities were nothing like those to which I, a rebellious and freewheeling teenager, was accustomed. The evening ended with a college student preaching and giving an invitation. His invitation was presented in these terms. "If you were killed in an auto accident on the way home (two months previously I had been seriously injured in an accident) and you woke up before the judgment seat of God, would God invite you into heaven?" Being a typical teen, I did not want to be different than everyone else, so I had one eye open to observe how I should respond. To my surprise, without hesitation most of my peers lifted their hands indicating "yes." I could not lift my hand because I was

---

[20] This wonderful opportunity for tens of thousands of other children was removed by the *wisdom* of the Supreme Court more than fifty years ago. On June 25, 1962, the United States Supreme Court decided in Engel v. Vitale that a prayer approved by the New York Board of Regents for use in schools violated the First Amendment by constituting an establishment of religion. The following year, in Abington School District v. Schempp, the Court disallowed Bible readings in public schools for similar reasons. These two landmark Supreme Court decisions centered on the place of religion in public education, and particularly the place of Protestantism, which had long been accepted as the given American faith tradition. Both decisions ultimately changed the face of American civil society, and in turn, helped usher in the last half-century of the culture wars. http://religionandpolitics.org/2012/06/25/when-the-court-took-on-prayer-the-bible-and-public-schools/ cited 12/18/17.

sure the answer for me was "no." That night I made a profession of faith and resolved to attend this Teenage Club.

On my first visit to the Teenage Club, I found 25-35 teens sitting on the showroom floor at the local Chevy dealership while the wife of the young couple led the group in singing choruses. She followed this by asking several teens to pray, and then she prayed. Her husband stood, opened a Bible while inviting the teens to open their Bibles, and proceeded to teach a passage from Scripture. I could understand him. The Bible made sense and life began to make sense.

Fast forward six years to my journey through seminary. Here is where I first encountered the word "worship" as a concept to understand. Up to this point worship was naively synonymous with what we did on Sunday mornings at church. But in seminary I began asking the question, "What is worship?" The answers were not satisfying. The study of church history did not enhance my understanding, since it seemed that each denomination had its own ideas and claimed they were the right ones.

One of my friends was a member of the Assembly of God denomination. He invited us to a service "to have a worship experience." My wife and I quickly concluded that if this was what it took to worship, we were not likely candidates to please God. (Don't take that comment as "put down" of my charismatic friends or their desire to worship. It is simply that this type of "worship" was outside of our comfort zone.)

During these years I led youth camps, church youth groups, and served on church staffs while attending seminary. I led youth meetings the way I observed my Teenage Club leaders leading them. But the question kept haunting me, "What is worship?" Later I was ordained in a good Southern Baptist Church under the leadership of Brother Paul R. Van Gorder and some years later migrated into the Presbyterian Church in America under the leadership of Rev. Jim Baird.

My wife and I enjoyed worship under Jim's leadership more than ever before. The wearing of robes, the use of more classical music, an integrated thematic service, and the more sermonic preaching all contributed to this experience. And yet, defining worship for us was elusive. The diversity of worship among my Reformed brothers was confusing.[21] That many spoke of *the elements of Reformed worship* as if there exists a clear stylistic formula did not clear up the confusion. The *culture wars or worship wars* of the past thirty years have not shed much light on the subject.

By now you must be saying, "OK. OK. So what does this Old Testament narrative have to do with defining worship?" Right question! So, let's have a look! What? You have another question? OK, bring it on. "Since we live in the New Testament Church, why are we looking at an Old Testament narrative to learn about

---

[21] Even in my own beloved denomination, The Presbyterian Church in America, one would be hard pressed to identify what worship is if one was to visit a church in New York, a church in Augusta, Georgia, and then a church in San Francisco. All would proclaim they practice Reformed worship but identifying the common elements for the average person would be difficult.

worship?" That is another great question. However, it has a simple answer. The Apostle Paul tells us that the Old Testament was written for our instruction. The New Testament assumes knowledge of the Old Testament. Hence, to understand the New Testament, one must study the Old Testament. And, frequently, the Old Testament illuminates the New Testament teachings with concrete illustrations.

There are many Old Testament passages to which we could turn for instruction on this matter of worship. However, one of the most beautiful is found in the narrative of 1 Chronicles 15-16. Chapter 15 recorded King David's moving of the Ark of the Covenant to Jerusalem.

In this chapter, we observe four principles that are important to organizing worship. The fifth and sixth principles are found in chapter 16. I am simply going to list these principles for your meditation because my focus is going to be on the dimensions of worship in chapter 16.

- It is important to lead worship according to the Bible (15:2, 13).
- Organization for worship is appropriate (15:1, 2, 25).
- Leaders are to model worship (15:27-29).
- God enables our worship (15:26).
- Worship leaders are important (16:7).

- Music is an essential element of corporate worship (16:4-6).[22]

The first observation is this. What is pictured in this narrative is corporate worship. In other narratives and in the Psalms, we find illustrations of personal worship and small group worship. However, what we find in these examples is subsumed in corporate worship.

The second observation is this. There are ten dimensions of worship in this narrative. Perhaps we could call these dimensions "elements." However, that word "elements" suggests necessary components. I am not convinced that every occasion of corporate worship must have all these dimensions to qualify as "true worship." Hence my use of the word "dimensions."

These are the dimensions of worship found in this narrative.

- Giving thanks to Him (16:8, 34).
- Singing to Him (16:9, 23).
- Speaking of His wonders (16:9b, 34).
- Rejoicing in Him—being glad (16:10).
- Seeking Him (16:11).
- Remembering His works (16:12, 15).

---

[22] Two observations about music may be useful. First, the type of instrument does not appear to be important. Here several are mentioned. Other places in the OT other instruments are mentioned. As culture changed and instruments developed it appears they were added to the repertoire of worship. The second observation is one that should please the younger generation and cause consternation to the older generation. It is found in 1 Chronicles 16:5 where we are told that the musicians played LOUD SOUNDING CYMBALS.

- Ascribing glory to Him (16:28).
- Trembling before Him (16:30-33).
- Praying to Him (16:35).
- Blessing Him (16:36).

Here, then, I have found the answer to my seminary question, "What is corporate worship?" Corporate worship is a congregation of believers joining together in a service organized according to the foregoing principles incorporating these dimensions in engaging with the Lord.[23]

Take note that these dimensions have as their object the Lord. The focus is not upon what the worshipper receives, but upon what the Lord receives. It is about Him and not the worshipper (not me). A colleague I asked to read this essay wrote:

> "The changes in worship styles over the last thirty to forty years have forced me to deal with myself more intentionally. By this I mean, coming to church thinking about someone other than myself (that is, 'what enables my pew-sharer to worship'), really concentrating on what I am doing during the worship service—that is worshipping God."[24]

---

[23] Notice that God (Him) is the focus. We are ascribing "worthship," the old English word for worship, to our God. Culture certainly colors the mode of expression, but God is the focus not the mode or a preference. Yes, I find formally organized worship very compatible with the glory and wonder of God as depicted from Genesis to Revelation. But formality does not guarantee worship any more than does emotion. It is the expression of our hearts through these dimensions unto the Lord that is worship.

[24] Dr. Howard E. Dial, while Pastor of Berachah Bible Church in Greater Atlanta, Georgia. Personal correspondence. May 2008.

These dimensions of worship are neither bound nor determined by culture. However, culture may impact how we practice expressing these dimensions. In recent years I have preached in a church that illustrates this point. When my wife and I entered the sanctuary just prior to the service, the musicians fascinated us. There was no piano. There was no organ. There was no brass. There were only three musicians with three instruments, a bass fiddle, a guitar, and a banjo. When they began to play the prelude, we realized that we were going to worship the old-fashioned country western style[25]. It certainly was different, but it also reminded me of my college days ministering in a mill town in North Carolina. The dimensions of worship were there but were certainly culturally framed.

This is not only true with music. I visited a Free Will Baptist Church in suburban Dallas while in graduate school. The preaching style was a falsetto voice with a definite rhythm. I purposefully focused on the content. On the drive home, I told my wife that I observed nothing inappropriate in his content, but that his style drove me crazy. She agreed.

If you are in the second half of your allotted three score and ten, it is going to be necessary for you to be sure that you are maturing in Christ and not fossilizing for Christ. I have served as the chairman of the Church and Pastoral Care Committee of my

---

[25] I have not visited one, but a rather recent phenomenon here in the south are Cowboy Churches. The church at which I preached was a Southern Baptist Church. I am assuming this would be the musical fair at a Cowboy Church along with western wear.

Presbytery.[26] In this role I have observed several churches diminish in membership because the old congregants found the worship style of the younger generation offensive (it is not what I want). Unfortunately, these older folks, more often than not, have fossilized. They have justified their personal historic preferences with baseless arguments. Unfortunately, their self-focus has weakened what was once a thriving body.

However, young people too often have synthesized their Christian beliefs with the secular musical model[27] and its concomitant casual life-style. They have prematurely fossilized in the process. The musical style, what they want, becomes more important than the welfare of the church. The casual life-style rejects any traditional formalism (liturgy). In the process, they simply invent their own liturgy: the raising of hands, the drums,

---

[26] For you non-Presbyterians, a Presbytery is a geographical sub-division of a national church. The ordained clergy in a Presbyterian church are members of this peer group who govern each other and who have responsibility for the local churches within its boundaries. This committee is charged with the pastoral care of both the clergy and the organized churches.

[27] I have come to the personal conclusion from the study of church history and brain science that the "worship wars" are a product of sociological patterning of the brain. In much the same way that the church gets one to three hours a week to influence child development in terms of conceptualization of life as compared to 109 to 112 hours a week for the world system, so it gets maybe 20 to 30 minutes as compared to 60 to 90 hours a week (depending on how much the young person is listening to an iPod or MTV) to establish musical patterns. If my understanding of brain science is correct, the more we think or experience a certain way the more we pattern our brain to conclude that what we are thinking or experiencing is correct. As the pattern is established, our brain more and more rejects anything that does not fit the pattern (becomes fossilized). Hence, it becomes important for each of us to listen to an outside source (the Bible as the Word of God) for us to course-correct and reprogram our brain where necessary. It is also incumbent upon us to recognize that Satan is always looking for a way to distract and confuse us.

and swaying with the rhythm, and the morning coffee cup in the pew. The focus again becomes "what I want" rather than the biblical dimensions of worship.[28]

We all have cultural comfort zones. Sometimes the Lord puts us in circumstances where it becomes necessary to expand that comfort zone to serve Him in a certain place. For most of you who read this volume, such an adjustment will not be necessary. You live in a country where you can find a congregation that fits within your comfort zone[29] and where these dimensions of worship characterize corporate worship. Find that place! Commit yourself to that congregation for the long duration. If, and when, the leadership of that congregation modifies congregational worship creating discomfort for you, ask yourself if the dimensions of worship remain in place. If so, seek to adjust to the cultural change. Don't fall prey to becoming "me-focused" in your worship. Adapt! Continue to serve the Lord in that congregation, contributing to the stability of God's work in that place and

---

[28] I had lunch recently with a high-ranking police officer. He related to me how the leadership of several churches in his jurisdiction interviewed the leadership of a rapidly growing church, that has spread like a local denomination over our state, to seek out the secret of their church growth. These churches have since installed smoke machines and other "gimmicks" found at rock concerts. This seems to be all about me (the worshiper) and not about worshiping God.

[29] "Comfort zone" here is not about "me," it is about focusing on the Lord in worship without being distracted by the cultural customs. I have the occasion to worship in African American churches of various denominations with some frequency. These are good churches that faithfully teach the Word. But some of the cultural practices are outside my comfort zone and I find myself needing to very consciously focus on the Lord in worship so as not to be distracted by my brethren's styles.

throughout the world where that congregation impacts the world for Christ.

Then all the people departed each to his house and David returned to bless his household (16:43). May reading this essay encourage you to leave worship and return home to bless your household because you engaged the Lord in worship and have been changed in the process.

~ ~ ~ ~ ~ ~ ~ ~ ~ ~ ~ ~

I asked my longtime colleague Dr. Howard Dial to read the first draft of this essay. Here is his response.

> "It kept my attention and speaks to issues that many face in our evangelical churches, especially older people. I have found that many of those over fifty or sixty can be very resistant to change. This is not really a surprise but only confirmed when it comes to worship styles, music, etc. You may want to address the older people and how maturing in Christ is not the same as fossilizing in Christ. Also of note, is that preferences in worship music tend to segregate themselves according to socio-economic class. There are exceptions of course. The changes in worship styles over the last thirty to forty years have forced me to deal with myself more intentional. By this I mean coming to church thinking about someone other than myself, and really concentrating on what I am doing during the

worship service. I mean really concentrating. I must be willing to forfeit some rights and preferences and be a worshiper all during the week. If all would experience the grace of the Spirit in our community or corporate worship, we would move more intimately into the unity of the Spirit in the bond of peace. Thanks for writing the piece. May God use it to prompt His people to a sweeter disposition about legitimate differences in our worship experience."

LIFE LESSON SEVEN

Worship is primarily about our God, and when we keep this focus, worship blesses our souls.

PERSONAL/COUNSELING/MENTORING APPLICATIONS

Personal: For the next four Sundays, monitor your thoughts regarding the dimensions of worship in your setting.
1. Do they fit the "check list" in this lesson?
2. What do you find distracting? Why?
3. Do you need an attitude adjustment?

Counseling/Mentoring: There are two situations in which this essay can be a useful contemplative assignment.
1. When counseling/mentoring a family in which there is conflict over concepts of worship?

2. When a counselee/mentoree has confided that he/she is considering withdrawing from a good evangelical church because of some changes in the worship style.
3. In the same manner, this would be a good book to give to a friend who has shared his frustration with his long-time church home over this issue. On the page provided at the beginning, write a note telling your friend to be sure to carefully read Life Lesson Seven.

Christianity is not a series of truths in the plural, but rather truth spelled with a capital "T." Truth about total reality, not just about religious things. Biblical Christianity is Truth concerning total reality—and the intellectual holding of that total Truth and then living in the light of that Truth.

~ Francis Schaeffer ~
Address at the University of Notre Dame,
Cited by Nancy Percy in
*Total Truth: Liberating Christianity from
Its Cultural Captivity*, p. 15

Life Lesson Eight

GENERATIONAL SURVIVAL DEPENDS UPON THE CREDIBILITY OF LEADERSHIP
1 Kings 11:1-11

In another essay I have written that community leadership has three key components. While other factors can contribute, I suggested that these three capture the essence of community leadership:

- Credibility—living what others expect (personal integrity—you walk what you talk).
- Wisdom—developed ability to work out principles in the public arena (application of knowledge to the contingencies of community life).
- Dependability—can be depended upon to rise to the occasion, whatever the need.

King Solomon certainly had wisdom. God clearly granted this to him when responding to Solomon's prayer. God said ... *I have done according to your words. Behold, I have given you a wise and discerning heart, so that there has been no one like you before you, nor shall one like you arise after you* (3:12). The wonderful example that we all remember is the story of the two prostitutes who lived together. They both had babies. During the night one accidentally smothered her child then exchanged her dead child for the other's living child. When they appear before Solomon for a judgment, he commanded that a sword be brought to divide the living child so that both mothers could have half the living child. To this horrific proposal, the mother of the living child cried out, "No, give her the living child." Solomon declared her to be the child's mother and placed the child in her custody (3:16-27).

Throughout the first nine chapters of the book of 2 Chronicles, it is demonstrated that Solomon possessed the third component of community leadership, dependability. Unfortunately, his community leadership was flawed by an ever-increasing loss of credibility. He did not live what God expected and in the process what the people expected. In the process, by his example, he led the people into the sins that destroyed the nation which David and Solomon had built by God's blessing.

History repeatedly witnesses the loss of credibility in leadership. The seeds of destruction are within; we live *credibly*, or we live *implausibly*. This principle is more obvious in a leader like Ahab, who flagrantly spurned the laws of God in his public and private life. When Jehoshaphat, the King of Judah, asks before engaging in a battle beside Ahab, *Is there not yet a prophet of the Lord here that we may inquire of him* Ahab answers, *There is one man by whom we may inquire of the Lord here, but I hate him because he does not prophesy good concerning me, but evil* (22:7-8). In chapter 21 we read that Elijah the Prophet had told Ahab, *I have found you, because you have sold yourself to do evil in the sight of the Lord ... acted very abominably in following idols, according to all the Amorites had done, whom the Lord cast out before the sons of Israel* (21:20, 26).

While the wisdom of Solomon was legendary, and his dependability unquestioned, his lack of credibility led to the same kind of community demise as did that of Ahab. Remember, credibility in this discussion means "living what others expect— you walk what you talk" (a constituent of personal leadership). At the inauguration of the temple Solomon led the people. He briefly stated the reason his father, David, had not built the temple. He offered a long and instructive prayer followed by a blessing of the people. He concluded the blessing with this exhortation: *Let your heart therefore be wholly devoted to the Lord our God, to walk in His statues and to keep His commandments, as at this day* (8:61). Surely, this exhortation would generate within the people the expectation that Solomon himself would live by it. They would expect credibility from their leader.

Solomon failed on three counts. As Moses was admonishing the people regarding their national character upon their entry into the Promised Land, he anticipated that the day would come when they would desire a king *like all the nations who are around* [us] (Deuteronomy 17:14-15). Through Moses, God gives four requisites of a king. First, he must be a countryman whom the Lord chooses. Second, he must not multiply horses for himself (especially from Egypt). Third, he must not multiply wives for himself (lest his heart turn away from God). Fourth, he must not increase the gathering of silver and gold for himself (Deuteronomy 17:15-18).

Solomon ultimately failed on three of those counts. The Scripture does not go into much detail with respect to Solomon's failure on two of the counts, but on the third, regarding wives, we find a significant passage in 1 Kings 11:1-11. Solomon did not live a credible life regarding women before God or the people. In fact, he exceedingly and flagrantly violated God's standard. The Scripture says he had 700 wives and 300 concubines and that these women *turned his heart away from the Lord and toward false gods* (11:7-8).

The result of this lack of credibility generated a flawed leadership that encouraged the people to engage in idolatry. The idolatry brought the demise of the kingdom. The result was a division of the kingdom into north and south, and the official establishment of an alternate religion in the northern kingdom. When leadership is not credible, it is destructive. We lack integrity if we make professions of faith in Christ, claim to be believers, and then live lives that are spotted with arrogant disregard for God's commandments. Such incongruity leads to family demise and community demise. Not only do we plant the seeds of destruction within our families and communities, but we invite God's judgment rather than His blessings (Isaiah 30:1).

The Deuteronomy passage gives us the key to living a credible life: self-immersion in the Word of God. Through Moses, God instructs the coming king when he writes,

> *Now it shall come about when he sits on the throne of his kingdom, he shall write for himself a copy of*

> *this law on a scroll in the presence of the Levitical priests. And it shall be with him and he shall read it all the days of his life, that he may learn to fear the Lord his God, by carefully observing all the word of this law and these statues, that his heart may not be lifted up above his countrymen and that he may not turn aside from the commandment, to the right or the left; in order that he and his sons may continue long in his kingdom in the midst of Israel*

(Deuteronomy 17:18-20).

The credibility of family and community leadership is marred with great regularity in our culture. On the peripheral edge we have the likes of Jim Jones and David Koresh. Much closer to the theological center we experience a Ted Haggard. Whatever your denominational or associational fellowship may be, a name or two of fallen leaders will pop into your mind as you are reading this. These people have been through the biblical training programs required for leadership. They have undergone the rigors of ordination. They have taken vows of purity both before the church and their mates. They study the Bible. They preach and teach. Yet, they destroy the credibility of their family and community. What happened to Solomon? What happened to those we know?

It seems to me that our answer is embedded in this Deuteronomy passage. Just what is it that Moses is prescribing as the insurance policy of credibility? There are four commands and there are four results when these commands are followed.

The first command is **personal engagement**. *He shall write for himself a copy of this law on a scroll* (Deuteronomy 17:18). A king in Israel was responsible for personal engagement with the Word of God. He was not to depend upon the religious leaders for his personal relationship with God. His writing of the copy of the law on a scroll would engage his total self in the process. Think about it! How would you like to copy the five books of Moses? Do you think you would have any better grasp of these books if you did?

The second command is **personal accountability**. The task of copying "this law" for himself was to be done in the presence of the priests. This accountability was intended to ensure accuracy, reverence, and integrity. In other words, it was intended to ensure that the task was done properly and in a timely manner. Furthermore, it ensured it was done in an environment where the king could comfortably ask questions and discuss his understanding of the meaning of the law as well as establish a relationship with the priests that would facilitate consultation during his reign. A very common practice of those who fail to "walk the talk" and thereby lose credibility is that they distance themselves from accountability.

The third command is **personal companioning**. *It shall be with him* (Deuteronomy 17:19). One weekend a fellow PCA minister was a guest in our home. Upon his arrival I was sitting in the living room working on my laptop. My wife greeted him at the door as I closed the laptop. As I stood he laughed and said, "The ever-present computer." This is the picture painted by Moses. If you were to unexpectedly step into the presence of the king, it should be of no surprise to find him consulting the Word of God. It was to be his companion.

The fourth command is **personal regularity**. *And, he shall read it all the days of his life* (Deuteronomy 17:19). He was not to be dependent upon the priests. He was to read it daily. How many teenagers observe their parents reading the Word on a daily basis? How many husbands and wives daily see one another reading the Word? The king was going to have the administration of a nation on his mind. He was going to have the temptations that accompany power. He was going to have the frustration of failure around him daily. He was going to have the burden of decisions throughout his day. He was going to need the refreshment, the warnings, the encouragement, the guidance that comes from God every day through His Word.

If the King of Israel was to take the time for such personal engagement with the Word of God daily, how can we conclude that we do not have the time for a walk with God? New Testament theology informs us that we are vice regents of Jesus Christ. We have God-given responsibilities. Surely, we need to personally and regularly engage with the Word of God in order that we might *stand, and having done all stand* (Ephesians 6:14).

There are four results promised to the king who would follow these instructions. The first is that **he would learn to love and fear God.** The Christian who engages in pornography or adultery is not close enough to God to either love or fear Him. Our sinful tendencies can be quickly enticed unless we are close enough to God to have a deep appreciation for His love that motivates us to purity, or close enough that our fear of His holiness kicks in to restrain us.

The second result is **protection from pride.** Moses describes this protection when he writes, *That his heart may not be lifted up above his countrymen* (Deuteronomy 17:20). The minister who enters an adulterous relationship is filled with pride. He thinks he deserves this sexual satisfaction while preaching righteousness to the congregation. Is this not what infected King David? He thought himself better than his commanders, so he did not go out into the battle with them. He looked upon Bathsheba and decided he deserved her although she was the wife of another. Pride in the form of "I deserve" leads to the loss of credibility in the family and the community.

The third result is **protection from deviation** ... *and that he may not turn aside from the commandment* (Deuteronomy 17:20). Keeping the Word of God as one's companion and consulting it daily will keep the king from either hardening his heart or developing pride. Notice that Moses adds to not turn aside *to the right or to the left* (Deuteronomy 17:20). Watching that occasional movie (for an ancient king, a belly dancer) that stirs lust is a slight step to the left; or, a slight step to the right of invoking legalism to generate assurance. Following the four commands in this passage will engender a touch of conviction by the Holy Spirit through the Word, enabling the king—or us—to resist this step to the left or to the right.

Finally, the fourth result is **the promise of blessings.** It is this ... *that he and his sons may live long in the kingdom.* His and his son's credibility will enhance their leadership and ensure the continuation of the kingdom. In the same manner, our following these instructions will enhance the lives of our families and our credibility for leadership in God's Kingdom.

Let us learn from a great king who failed to follow through on God's insurance policy. Let us be careful to engage the Word of God with a framework of accountability. Let us make the Word of God our companion and consult it daily. Let us pray that God will grant us credible leadership in our families and our communities so that our children and their children after us will glorify God and enjoy His blessings.

Life Lesson Eight

We live credibly, or we live implausibly.

Personal/Counseling/Mentoring Applications

There are three types of counselees/mentorees that come to mind immediately who could profit from reading this essay.

1. The husband who struggles to read and to study the Word of God with regularity.
2. The church leader who protests that he is so busy that he cannot find the time to regularly engage the Word of God.

3. The arrogant individual who thinks he can handle life just fine with occasional church attendance.

Here is a very simple and powerful solution for all three categories.

- Plan/schedule a time to personally and formally engage with God in His Word.
- Communicate your plan to your spouse or trusted friend with the charge and permission to once a week ask you straight up: "Have you kept your schedule to meet with God this week?"
- Third, each day record one lesson or challenge or observation that strikes you and thank God for it.
- When you fail (and you will), refuse to be defeated. Seek God's forgiveness for not keeping your promise, accept that forgiveness, and get back on track.

Life Lesson Nine

Five Lessons for Leaders & One Pitfall to Avoid

2 Chronicles 29-33

One morning after my quiet time I wrote this letter to my son and my son-in-law. Over the years this has become a frequent practice. At other times, the product of my meditation that is deemed useful for counseling has been sent to my counseling staff for use in their practice.

To my dear sons:

I was visiting with my Old Testament characters again this morning in my time with the Lord. The man of the day was Hezekiah (2 Chronicles 29-33). It is somewhat surprising that five full chapters are given to this "late-in-the-game" king of Judah. There are some great lessons on leadership in these passages. There are some great lessons on persistence. There are some great lessons on trusting God. And there is one big lesson on the consequences of pride (32:22-31). However, the lesson that really struck me was in chapter 33 verses one and two.

Being a great spiritual public leader is dangerous for your family. Whatever God calls you to do, whatever your leadership opportunities, remember to lead your family first. I sometimes paraphrase a question posed by Jesus, *For what shall it profit a man, if he shall gain the whole world, and lose his own soul?* (Mark 8:36 KJV) to read, "What shall it profit a man if he shall gain the whole world and lose his own family?"

Manasseh was twelve years old when he became king, and he reigned fifty-five years in Jerusalem .... And he did evil in the sight of the Lord according to the abominations of the nations whom the Lord dispossessed before the sons of Israel. (2 Kings 21:1-2 ESV).

But first, five lessons for leaders from the life of Hezekiah and then one pitfall for parents to avoid.

Five Lessons for Leaders

Lesson number one: **When you are given a role as leader** (whether the teacher of the three-year old Sunday School, elected to the eldership of your church, or the United States Senate), **begin with the revitalization of your spiritual life.** This is what Hezekiah did. Here is what we read. *In the first year of his reign, in the first month, he opened the doors of the house of the LORD and repaired them* (29:3 ESV).

Lesson number two: **Call together all those under your leadership and challenge them to "consecrate" themselves and to** *consecrate the house of the LORD* **by cleaning out the filth** (29:4-5). For you and me and all those under our leadership, the house of the Lord is our individual bodies and the collective corporate body in our gathered local church. In some cases, it may also include cleaning out the junk from the church building to facilitate worship and the work of the Lord.

Unfortunately, the evangelical church today is cluttered with a lot of junk—superfluous feel-good nonsense that at best keeps some folks attending and at worse becomes idols that replace the living God. Then there are the immoral sexual practices that are so prevalent. If the statistics are accurate, three in five men sitting in the pew of the average church on Sunday morning are engaging in pornography. In the late 1940s college students waited till the third date to kiss. Today, by the third date, you are expected to sleep together.[30] Divorcees have tasted sexual satisfaction and carry on life as usual.

I trust you will challenge those around you as well as lead an exemplary life before them. As leaders you cannot sit quietly back and ignore the condition of the church. You need to be part of the clarion call to repentance (cleaning out the filth). Those practicing these abominable lifestyles must be encouraged to consecrate themselves as the *house of the LORD*, the body of Christ.[31]

---

[30] Several years ago, a 30-something young woman came to see me. After some polite conversation she said, "I have just one question I need to have you answer." I nodded, and she continued. "I have dated deacons from three different churches in three different denominations in the past year. In each case, on the third dinner date, it was plainly communicated that I was expected to sleep with them." My question is, "Do I have to do this to acquire a husband?" Sadly, she was very serious.

[31] See Paul's instructions to the Church at Corinth in 1 Corinthians [sic]. He uses very forthright language.

Lesson number three follows logically from lesson two: **repentance!** Hear what the Chronicler records: *For our fathers have been unfaithful and have done what was evil in the sight of the* L{\scriptsize ORD} *our God* (29:6 ESV). Unfaithfulness that was not engaging in regular private and public worship had become the rule, not the exception. They were a nation of professing believers who lived pagan lives. Any pastor called to a city or suburban church will quickly recognize this malady in his congregation. As a pastor friend observed one day in my hearing, "On any given Lord's Day I can count on two-thirds of my people being present, but on most of those days it is seldom the same two-thirds. They rotate between the mountains, the shore, and the pew."

They also shut the doors of the vestibule and put out the lamps and have not burned incense or offered burnt offerings in the Holy Place to the God of Israel (29:7 ESV) is the second evil to which Hezekiah draws attention and which requires repentance. When I was church planting (in the 1970s), it was expected that as the pastor/leader I would provide a substantial Bible study on Wednesday evenings and preach twice on Sundays. Those expectations are gone. In most, even *solid* evangelical churches today, if there is a mid-week meeting and a Sunday evening service it is at the initiation of the pastor and measured by the absence of many, and they are not the expectation of the congregation.

As a leader in whatever role in our current cultural context, it is important to call people to repentance for their neglect of worship.

Lesson number four: **Fearless prophetic proclamation regarding judgment is observed from the leadership of Hezekiah.** He points to the culture and notes the judgment of God in process. Here are his words:

> *Therefore the wrath of the* LORD *came on Judah and Jerusalem, and he has made them an object of horror, of astonishment, and of hissing, as you see with your own eyes. For behold, our fathers have fallen by the sword, and our sons and our daughters and our wives are in captivity for this* (29:8-9 ESV).

What he did was not politically correct! In his case, he had the absolute power of kingship, but it does not mean that what he did, said, or called for was popular with the *establishment*. If he had been the President rather than the King, no doubt he would have suffered public abuse like that suffered by an American President who calls on the establishment to change. The reading of these chapters that cover his reign demonstrates, on a very practical level, the benefits of leadership that steps up to the plate and calls professing believers to spiritual renewal. Regardless of the level of the role of leadership, this principle is essential. Every organization and every individual life is subject to the spiritual law of thermodynamics (energy tends to migrate into entropy).³²

Hezekiah was practicing that to which both Paul and James call us in their New Testament writings. Listen: *Brothers and sisters, if someone is caught in a sin, you who live by the Spirit should restore that person gently. But watch yourselves, or you also may be tempted* (Galatians 6:1 NIV). There can be no question that James is on the same page: *My brothers and sisters, if one of you should wander from the truth ... someone should bring that person back* (James 5:19 NIV). Israel, the people and leadership, had wandered from where they should have been and were stuck in their sin. Hezekiah is practicing spiritual leadership. He is working to restore them and set them back on the path of righteousness and blessing.

Lesson number five: **There is another very important lesson from the life of Hezekiah that leaders cannot afford to miss.** It is this: our cultivation of revival among our followers does not ensure that we are not

---

[32] Why is it that when you leave an ice cube at room temperature, it begins to melt? Why do we get older and never younger? And, why is it whenever rooms are cleaned, they become messy again in the future? Certain things happen in one direction and not the other; this is called the "arrow of time" and it encompasses every area of science. The thermodynamic arrow of time (entropy) is the measurement of disorder within a system. Denoted as ΔS, the change of entropy suggests that time itself is asymmetric with respect to order of an isolated system, meaning: a system will become more disordered, as time increases.
https://chem.libretexts.org/Core/Physical_and_Theoretical_Chemistry/Thermodynamics/Laws_of_Thermodynamics/Second_Law_of_Thermodynamics --Cited 10-08-17

vulnerable to sin. Hezekiah embraced the sin of pride. In chapter thirty-two the account of his pride is recorded. His spiritual faithfulness led to multiple blessings. His leadership generated a strong nation and a healthy economy at God's hand. *And many brought gifts to the Lord to Jerusalem and precious things to Hezekiah king of Judah, so that he was exalted in the sight of all nations from that time onward* (32:23 ESV). Then Hezekiah became sick. He pled with the Lord for healing. God granted him more years.

It is interesting that his pride seems to emanate initially from the fact that God healed him. It is reminiscent of the boy who is prouder of the fact that he has been a good boy than of his new bicycle his parents gave him because he had been humble and obedient. *In those days Hezekiah became sick and was at the point of death, and he prayed to the Lord, and he answered him and gave him a sign. But Hezekiah did not make return according to the benefit done to him, for his heart was proud* (32:24-25 ESV). Hezekiah's healing drew the attention of foreign emissaries bearing congratulatory gifts. His response was a prideful display of his great riches implying that he took credit for the wealth.

Since God invested so much of His Word in presenting the life of Hezekiah, it is worth our time to consider each of the five prior lessons and how they might impact us today.

And now my sons consider **one pitfall for parents to avoid**. In God's Providence He has populated both of your families with incredible children for whom you bear the responsibility to raise them in the *nurture and admonition of the Lord* (Ephesians 6:4 NIV).

When we read about the wonderful revivals under Hezekiah, we cannot but be struck by these two verses. How is it that a king about whom it is written, *Every work which he began in the service of the house of God in law and in commandment, seeking his God, he did with all his heart and prospered* (31:21), should end up with a successor son of whom it is written, *he did evil in the sight of the Lord ...* (33:2)? While it is not all the answer, I think here is much of the answer.

Hezekiah failed to recognize that a child's natural bent is toward evil! **Godly men are often so occupied with serving God and creating wealth** (felt responsibility to provide for their families at best, or selfish gain for themselves at worst) **that they neglect to forge a son's heart.** I have heard that Bertram Russell, atheistic British philosopher of the 20th century observed that, "Every generation is only one generation from barbarianism, so that every generation must civilize the next generation." He came close. The fact is that every generation is evil, so that every generation must be converted and discipled into humble submission to the living God.

My dear sons don't miss the reality of this pitfall! Between you there are nine precious lives to be discipled. Pam and I can help, as can the other grandparents, but you are the leaders. I would desire success for both of you. I would desire reasonable wealth for both of you. But, in the pursuit of success (in ministry or business), be careful that you neglect not the greater task of discipleship.

Hezekiah, I believe, failed Manasseh on two fronts. There is no record of his investing in discipling his son as he did the priests and Levites, and secondly, he was preoccupied with amassing wealth (which probably also spoiled his son and led to his arrogance). Both these activities left him precious little time and energy for discipling his son. The discipleship of our children is a matter of intentionality. It is teaching and living out Deuteronomy 6:4-9.

This Deuteronomy passage is the clearest and most concise instruction found anywhere in the Bible regarding transferring the faith from one generation to the next. Discipleship of children flows through nurture. Nurturing takes time, energy, forethought, prayerfulness, playfulness, affection, and as seen in the Deuteronomy passage, both formal and informal instruction.

Unfortunately, the generations of life are littered with the broken lives of children whom parents loved but did not parent. I urge you to emulate Hezekiah's spiritual commitments, but, apply them first to your own families. Avoid this pitfall!

Life Lesson Nine

The greatest opportunity for evangelism, transferring the faith as well as character development from one generation to the next, resides in the Christian home.

Personal/Counseling/Mentoring Applications

1. If you are a parent, create a check list for yourself of these six lessons and then evaluate your parenting based upon them. Then ask yourself, "What changes do I need to make?"
2. If you are a grandparent, prayerfully consider acquiring a copy of this book for your children or just give them your copy and ask them to read this letter.
3. If you are counseling, mentoring, or discipling a young couple, assign this chapter and then discuss it with them.

Life Lesson Ten

DISPLAYING THE LOVING KINDNESS OF GOD
Psalm 107

Lesson Introduction

The style of this last chapter is radically different. As I was reading Psalm 107 one morning, it suddenly burst into a set of scenes. I grabbed a pen and began scratching out the scenes. From that point on it was a matter of meditatively refining both the thought process and the schema, which eventually became a five-act play. I choose the word "play" over "scene"[33] because they are a series of stories with scenes that make up a whole play (Psalm) that has one theme.

The Psalm divides into five parts (acts). Four of these parts describe the four occurrences of Israelite journeys as they return to their land.[34] The struggles of life and the failure to keep their focus on God with the resultant departures from God's prescribed ways are depicted. The appending discipline and deliverance by the Lord leads to the refrain that is the point of the Psalm. The fifth part (act) is a recapitulation of all that goes before, setting forth with

---

[33] An act is often defined as the major division of drama, and it forms the basic structure of a performance. An act is very long because it is a collection of different scenes that flow together, and it establishes a major part of the story. Read more: Difference Between Scene and Act | Difference Between http://www.differencebetween.net/language/words-language/difference-between-scene-and-act/#ixzz53EOQaaQ3

[34] See *The Treasury of David* cited in:
https://www.biblestudytools.com/commentaries/treasury-of-david/psalms-107-1.html

great clarity the folly of autonomy and the blessing of submission to the King.

The 17th century commentator, Adam Clarke (1760-1832) cites Robert Lowth (1710-1787) as observing that,

> "No doubt the composition of this psalm is admirable throughout; and the descriptive part of it adds at least its share of beauty to the whole; but what is but most to be admired is its conciseness, and withal the expressiveness of the diction, which strikes the imagination with inimitable elegance. The weary and bewildered traveller, the miserable captive in the hideous dungeon, the sick dying man, the seaman foundering in a storm, are described in so affecting manner, that they far exceed anything of the kind, though never so labored. I may add that had such an Idyll appeared in Theocritus or Virgil or had it been found as a scene in any of the Greek tragedians, even in Aeschylus himself, it would probably have been produced as their master piece."

To the best of my knowledge, I had never read Clarke on Psalm 107. This passage simply turned up as I was reading in preparation to write this introduction. It is evident that I am not the first person to be struck with the theatrical possibilities of this passage. We should not be surprised, since the Psalm was written by King David,[35] who, along with all his other gifts, was a literary genius.

Now, a few words about King David. First, **he was anointed as the second King of Israel** after the first, Saul, was rejected by God (neither the practical nor the theological reasons are pertinent here, just the fact). There were likely some twenty years of turmoil for David living under Saul's reign (see 1 Samuel 16 through 2 Samuel 2). God was using those years to refine, season, and prepare David for kingship.

Second, **David was an ancient prophet.** Peter, an Apostle, declares this so in Acts 2:29-31 (KJV). Here is what Peter says as he addresses a Jewish audience of laymen and scholars:

> *Men and brethren, let me speak freely to you of the patriarch David, that he is both dead and buried, and his tomb is with us to this day. Therefore, being a prophet, and knowing that God had sworn with an oath to him that of the fruit of his body, according to the flesh, He would raise up the Christ to sit on his throne, he, foreseeing this, spoke concerning the resurrection of the Christ, that His soul was not left in Hades, nor did His flesh see corruption. This Jesus God has raised up, of which we are all witnesses.*

---

[35] Zenger, Erich (1998). "The Composition and Theology of the Fifth Book of Psalms, Psalms 107-145". *Journal for the Study of the Old Testament* (80): 77–102.

Third, **David is the designated progenitor of both the blood line of Jesus**[36] **and the physical kingship to which Jesus will ascend.**[37]

Hence, David the prophet, writing with his artistic bent, is a wonderful way to bring this short volume to a conclusion. Let your imagination see the play unfold as you read the script.

---

[36] See the genealogies in Matthew 1 and Luke 3.
[37] Psalm 22:28 is the prophetic word. See Romans 14:11; Philippians 2:10; Zechariah 9:9; Revelation 19:11-16.

DISPLAYING THE LOVING KINDNESS OF GOD
A FIVE ACT PLAY
Psalm 107

Stage Directions: Curtain rolls back revealing a completely black stage. As a choir sings verses 1-3 (ESV) the lights come up with a bright spot focusing on the narrator who is dressed in a black robe.

Oh give thanks to the Lord, for he is good,
> *for his steadfast love endures forever!*
Let the redeemed of the Lord say so,
> *whom he has redeemed from trouble*
and gathered in from the lands,
> *from the east and from the west,*
from the north and from the south.

Narrator: I invite you to engage your imagination. The only voices you will hear are soliloquies, the voice of God, and mine. Some actors will deliver soliloquies while some will pantomime their roles. You will need to tune your ears to hear the story and you will need to see what the words depict.

Act I

Psalm 107:4-9

Narrator: This first act depicts man in his lost condition. It does not depict man as consciously choosing to be rebellious, but rather as a lost child who cannot find his way home. And, like a lost child, his fear at the realization that he is lost brings tears through which he calls out for his Daddy (verse 6). This is followed by the simple description of the actions of God (NKJV).

> *They wandered in the wilderness in a desolate way;*
>> *They found no city to dwell in.*
> *Hungry and thirsty,*
>> *Their soul fainted in them.*
> *Then they cried out to the Lord in their trouble,*
>> *And He delivered them out of their distresses.*
> *And He led them forth by the right way,*
>> *That they might go to a city for a dwelling place.*
> *Oh, that men would give thanks to the Lord for His goodness,*
>> *And for His wonderful works to the children of men!*
> *For He satisfies the longing soul,*
>> *And fills the hungry soul with goodness.*

Stage Directions: An actor comes onto the stage that depicts a near eastern wilderness. He displays distress and fear as he scrambles aimlessly in one direction and then another.

The actor utters a soliloquy based upon verses 4-5a.

"I have wandered in the wilderness—this awful desert region. I have searched tirelessly for community—for an inhabited city. I long for food, my tongue is parched with thirst and my soul is in despair."

The Voice of God: "Come my son, I will lead you straightway to an inhabited city."

Stage Directions: The lights dim as the actor exits with hands lifted in praise.

Narrator [based upon verses 8-9]: "Let them give thanks to the Lord for His lovingkindness and for the wonders that he displays to the sons of men. For He satisfies their thirsty souls, He brings fullness to their hungry souls, giving them what is good."

Act II
Psalm 107:10-16

Narrator: "Unlike the lost child of Act One, the second act focuses on a group of individuals who depict rebels. A motorcycle gang, chains, bandana head coverings, and attitudes depicted by surly faces are milling around a decrepit motorcycle shop façade on one side of the stage while a grave yard is on the other side. The scene is on a dark night, with a yellowy quarter moon and threatening clouds moving quickly."

Actors: As the gang is milling around, one member raises a clenched fist and shakes it toward the heavens. Suddenly, there is a lightning strike and the shop bursts into flames.

Narrator [based upon verses 10-12]: "There are those who dwell in darkness, living in the shadow of death. They are prisoners of misery of their own making. They are held in self-imposed chains because they choose to ignore the Word of God and spurn His counsel in exchange for their own counsel."

The Voice of God: "Oh, rebellious people. I have humbled you to help you see your need for Me."

Actors: These hard men in unison fall upon their knees and lift their hands toward the heavens as they chant [based upon verse

13a]: "Oh, Lord God, we are in trouble, we have attempted to be our own God."

The Voice of God responds to their repentance [based upon verses 13b-14]: "I have saved you from your distress. I have translated you from the kingdom of darkness into the kingdom of light. When you humbled yourselves, you saw My hand delivering you from your distresses."

Action on the Set: Rain puts out the fire. The dark clouds disappear and are replaced with a full moon and sky full of stars.

The Voice of God: "I have brought you out of darkness and delivered you from the pathway of eternal death. I have broken the bonds of your sin. You must no longer live in rebellion. I, the Lord, have delivered you!"

Narrator [based upon verses 15-16]: "Now watch these humble, repentant men give thanks to God for His lovingkindness for they have seen wonders and praise Him before the congregation."

Act III
Psalm 107:17-22

Action on the Set: The backdrop is that of an Elizabethan banquet room with several courtier fools aimlessly running around the banquet table with the king and his court enjoying the banquet.

Narrator: As the actors engage, the narrator says [based upon verses 17-18]: "They are fools to practice their rebellious ways. They are afflicted because of their choices. They are so distressed that they abhor the enjoyment and nourishment of food that the King has graciously provided. Their lifestyle drives them more and more toward the grave."

Actors: The fools, dressed as 16th century court jesters, are acting out their rejection of the food while limping and showing weakness (see verses 17-18). After portraying their rejection of the food and getting weaker and weaker, they fall down and lift their empty hands toward the heavens and bow their heads (see verse 19a), one, then another, then another, until all six have dropped to their knees.

The Voice of God [based upon verses 19b-20] and a quote from another prophet (Jeremiah 17:4 ESV): "I have saved you from your distresses by sending you My Word to heal you and deliver you from your own destructiveness. You have prayed Jeremiah's prayer when he was in deep distress not because of his rebellion, but because of his faithfulness. Jeremiah cried out, *Heal me, O LORD, and I will be healed; Save me and I will be saved, for you are my praise*, and you being fools like those who persecuted Jeremiah, have cried out and I will save you by My Word as I did Jeremiah."

Narrator's refrain [based upon verses 21-22]: "Come, ye fools, give thanks to the Lord for His lovingkindness. Give thanks for the wonder of His redemptive love that cannot be earned, but only responded to. Offer sacrifices of thanksgiving and witness to His works of love with joyful singing."

Actors: All rise to their feet. They lift their hands in worship and with one voice shout: "Praise God from whom all blessings flow!"

Act IV
Psalm 107:23-32

Action on the Set: The backdrop is a swirling ocean driven by the wind with a 1st century ship bobbing like a cork.

Actors: Six rough sailors simulate standing on the deck of the bobbing ship struggling to stay upright while reeling like drunken men.

Narrator: "I am Paul, who informed you that my God has told me we will survive, but you must stay on board the ship. If you continue to rebel, refuse to listen, and depart the ship, all shall be lost."

The Voice of God [based upon verses 28-29]: "Wind, be still! You have cried out in your distress and I have stilled the wind. As you see, the waves of the sea have calmed. I will guide you to your safe-haven."

Narrator [based upon verses 31-32]:
"These rough and rebellious sailors who thought they were going to sail God's world without Him found themselves on the brink of disaster; but God, pushing them beyond their limits brought them to repentance and delivered them by His Word. Now they give thanks for His lovingkindness, having been amazed by the wonder

of His work. They glorify Him before the people of God and they give praise before the elders as they come into the fellowship of God's people."

Actors: Standing before a crowd, they act out their deliverance, amazement, and praise as the lights dim out.

Act V

Psalm 107:33-42

Action on the Set: This act is different. It does not start with actors, but rather as the narrator speaks, the stage lights move from scene to scene depicting what he describes.

First Scene: There is a beautiful river running through an oasis dotted with fruitful vegetation.

Narrator [reads verse 33 NKJV]:
> *He turns rivers into a wilderness,*
> *And the water springs into dry ground;*

Second Scene: There is a dying landscape with an actress dressed in scarlet sitting by the door of her house and a man approaching her.

Narrator [reads verse 34 NKJV]:
> *A fruitful land (is turned) into barrenness,*
> *For the wickedness of those who dwell in it.*

Third Scene: The lights return to the first scene, with the addition of a city on the edge of the oasis, with actors approaching the city,

Narrator [reads verses 35-38 NKJV]:

> *He turns a wilderness into pools of water,*
> *And dry land into water springs.*
> *There He makes the hungry dwell,*
> *That they may establish a city for a dwelling place,*
> *And sow fields and plant vineyards,*
> *That they may yield a fruitful harvest.*
> *He also blesses them, and they multiply greatly;*
> *And He does not let their cattle decrease.*

Fourth Scene: All lights come up so that all scenes are visible.

Narrator (reads the following paraphrase of verses 39-42): "When the people rebel and play the fool, God, once again in His love, visits them with oppression, misery, and sorrow by making them wander in the pathless wasteland as their ungodly leaders have led them away from the worship of God. In His lovingkindness He cares for the needy, the faithful of the family of God. He shepherds when His shepherds fail to shepherd them."

Action on the Set: Stage goes dark for 45 seconds and is cleared of all but two tablets of stone.

Fifth Scene: In the background there is an increasing roll of thunder, then a splitting lightning flash immediately followed by a bright and focused spotlight on the tablets of stone—The Ten Commandments.

Narrator [based upon verse 43]: "Who is wise? Let him give heed to these things! Let him consider the lovingkindness of the Lord!"

Stage goes dark as either "Amazing Grace" or "It Is Well with My Soul" fades in; the stage stays dark while the scene of the oasis with the city is put in place. With the stage setting completed the light gradually comes up to fullness by the last verse of the hymn.

LIFE LESSON TEN

To our God, Christian living is serious business. It is the lovingkindness of the Lord that disciplines us to repentance so that we might embrace the law of the Lord and find the fullness of life He desires us to experience.

PERSONAL/COUNSELING/MENTORING APPLICATIONS

The life takeaway here is simple, but profound. God's rules are for our benefit. They keep us in fellowship with Him. They keep us in fellowship with each other. In short, they enable us to glorify God and enjoy Him forever.

About the Author

Dr. Howard Eyrich's career has spanned more than sixty years. He has filled various roles including seminary professor and president, pastor and church planter. He retired as the Director of Counseling Ministries at Briarwood Presbyterian Church, Birmingham, Alabama.

He has served on the boards of the Association of Certified Biblical Counselors, Birmingham Theological Seminary, Trinity Seminary, and the Biblical Counseling Coalition, and The Owen Center as well as various Presbytery and Presbyterian Church in America denominational committees, to name the major efforts.

His publishing efforts include two books as solo author, three books with a co-author, and numerous chapters in significant volumes in the biblical counseling field, as well as articles for *The Journal of Biblical Counseling* and several other magazines.

Dr. Eyrich and his wife Pamela have two grown children, eight grandchildren and one great-grandchild. Retirement for him is a time for ministry. He writes, teaches, preaches, and travels for the kingdom. He also enjoys the hobbies of model railroading, hunting, and shooting.

Dr. Eyrich is available to speak in conferences, fill pulpits, and for intensive marriage interventions, especially with ministries couples.

Follow Howard Eyrich

Facebook: facebook.com/howardeyrich

Twitter: Howard Eyrich @earkie1

Instagram: Howard Eyrich @earkie1

Amazon: http://amzn.to/2wSR9FF

Blog: howardeyrich.com

ALSO BY THE AUTHOR

A Call to Christian Patriotism: A Weekly Devotional Essay Series – Howard A. Eyrich, Focus Publishing, Bemidji, MN, 2012.

After an Affair: Rebuilding Your Trust; Rebuilding Your Marriage—Howard Eyrich & Cheryl Blackmon. Growth Advantage Communication, 2016.

Christian Decision Making and the Will of God: A Practical Model – Howard Eyrich, KDP, 2014

Curing the Heart: A Model for Biblical Counseling – Howard Eyrich & William Hines, Christian Focus Publications, 2014.

Grief: Learning to Live with Loss – Howard A. Eyrich, P & R Publishing, 2010

Hope and Help for the Homosexual – Howard Eyrich & Howard Dial, Focus Publishing, Bemidji, MN, 2011.

Hope and Help for the Suffering – Howard Eyrich & Howard Dial, Focus Publishing, Bemidji, MN, 2010.

Hope for New Beginnings—Dr. Howard Eyrich and Shirley Crowder, Growth Advantage Communication LLC, 2017.

Paul the Counselor: Disciple-making as Modeled by the Apostle – edited by Bill Hines & Mark Shaw (Chapters 7 & 12), Focus Publishing, Bemidji, MN, 2014.

The Art of Aging: A Christian Handbook – Howard Eyrich, – Howard A. Eyrich, Focus Publishing, Bemidji, MN, 2012.

Three to Get Ready: Premarital Counseling Manual, 2nd Edition – Howard Eyrich, Focus Publishing, Bemidji, MN, 1996.

Totally Sufficient: The Bible and Christian Counseling, Revised – Ed Hindson & Howard Eyrich, Christian Focus Publishing, 2004.

Scripture References

OLD TESTAMENT

Genesis 2:23-25	p 36	Psalm 51	p 51
Exodus 17	p 45	Psalm 107	
Numbers 4:15	p 75		pp 111, 112 & 115
Numbers 20	p 45	Psalm 107:1-3	p 115
Numbers 20:8-12	p 46	Psalm 107:4-5	p 117
Numbers 20:10-11	p 45	Psalm 107:4-9	p 116
Numbers 27:14	p 46	Psalm 107:6	p 116
Deuteronomy 6:1-10	p 22	Psalm 107:8-9	p 117
Deuteronomy 6:4-9	p 109	Psalm 107:10-12	p 118
Deuteronomy 17:14-15		Psalm 107:10-16	p 118
	p 93	Psalm 107:13	p 119
Deuteronomy 17:15-18		Psalm 107:13-14	p 119
	P 93	Psalm 107:15-16	p 119
Deuteronomy 17:18	p 96	Psalm 107:17-18	p 120
Deuteronomy 17:18-20		Psalm 107:17-22	p 120
	p 95	Psalm 107:19-20	p 120
Deuteronomy 17:19		Psalm 107:21-22	p 121
	pp 96 & 97	Psalm 107:23-32	p 122
Deuteronomy 17:20	p 98	Psalm 107:28-29	p 122
Psalm 22:28	p 114	Psalm 107:31-32	p 122
Psalm 32	p 51	Psalm 107:33	p 124
Psalm 37:8	p 16	Psalm 107:33-42	p 124
Psalm 38	p 51	Psalm 107:34	p 124

Psalm 107:35-38	p 125	1 Samuel 3:19	p 68
Psalm 107:39-42	p 125	1 Samuel 3:20	p 68
Psalm 107:43	p 126	1 Samuel 3:21	p 68
Proverbs 5	p 46	1 Samuel 4	p 67
Ecclesiastes 9:10	p 53	1 Samuel 4:1	p 68
Isaiah 30:11	p 94	1 Samuel 4:3	p 69
Isaiah 55:8-9	p 72	1 Samuel 4:1-5	p 67
Jeremiah 17:4	p 120	1 Samuel 4:4-11	p 70
1 Samuel 1	pp 36 & 67	1 Samuel 4:8	p 71 & 73
1 Samuel 1:1-28	p 35	1 Samuel 5	pp 67 & 73
1 Samuel 1:4	p 37	1 Samuel 5:1-5	p 67
1 Samuel 1:6	p 37	1 Samuel 5:3	pp 73 & 74
1 Samuel 1:8	p 38	1 Samuel 5:7	p 73
1 Samuel 1:10	p 39	1 Samuel 5:9	p 74
1 Samuel 1:10-11	p 39	1 Samuel 5:10	p 74
1 Samuel 1:14	p 40	1 Samuel 5:11	p 74
1 Samuel 1:17	p 40	1 Samuel 6	p 67
1 Samuel 1:27-28	p 67	1 Samuel 6:1-2	p 74
1 Samuel 2	p 67	1 Samuel 6:4-18	p 74
1 Samuel 2:1-11	p 35	1 Samuel 6:19	p 75
1 Samuel 2:12	p 67	1 Samuel 16	p 113
1 Samuel 2:17-25	p 67	1 Samuel 17	p 113
1 Samuel 2:22	p 67	1 Samuel 18	p 113
1 Samuel 2:32-34	p 68	1 Samuel 19	p 113
1 Samuel 2:32-35	p 67	1 Samuel 20	p 113
1 Samuel 3:15-18	p 68	1 Samuel 21	p 113

1 Samuel 22	p 113	1 Kings 11:7-8	p 94
1 Samuel 23	p 113	1 Kings 18:18-46	p 59
1 Samuel 24	p 113	1 Kings 21	p 58
1 Samuel 25	p 113	1 Kings 21:20	p 92
1 Samuel 26	p 113	1 Kings 21:26	p 92
1 Samuel 27	p 113	1 Kings 22	p 58
1 Samuel 28	p 113	1 Kings 22:7-8	p 92
1 Samuel 29	p 113	2 Kings 21:1-2	p 102
1 Samuel 30	p 113	**1 Chronicles** 15	
1 Samuel 31	p 113		pp 27, 77 & 81
2 Samuel 1	p 113	1 Chronicles 15:1	p 81
2 Samuel 2:1-2	p 113	1 Chronicles 15:2	p 81
2 Samuel 11	p 45	1 Chronicles 15:13	p 81
2 Samuel 11:1	p 46	1 Chronicles 15:25	p 81
2 Samuel 11:1-2	pp 46 & 51	1 Chronicles 15:26	p 81
2 Samuel 11:2	p 48	1 Chronicles 15:27-29	p 81
2 Samuel 11:3	pp 47 & 51	1 Chronicles 16	
2 Samuel 11:4	p 52		pp 27, 77 & 81
2 Samuel 11:6	p 52	1 Chronicles 16:4-6	p 82
2 Samuel 11:15	p 52	1 Chronicles 16:5	p 82
2 Samuel 11:27	pp 50 & 53	1 Chronicles 16:7	p 80 & 81
2 Samuel 12:7	p 51	1 Chronicles 16:8	p 82
1 Kings 3:12	p 91	1 Chronicles 16:9	p 82
1 Kings 3:16-27	p 92	1 Chronicles 16:10	p 82
1 Kings 8:61	p 93	1 Chronicles 16:11	p 82
1 Kings 11:1-11	pp 91 & 94	1 Chronicles 16:12	p 82

1 Chronicles 16:15	p 82	2 Chronicles 17:10-11	p 57
1 Chronicles 16:23	p 82	2 Chronicles 17:12-19	p 57
1 Chronicles 16:28	p 83	2 Chronicles 17:29	p 61
1 Chronicles 16:30-33	p 83	2 Chronicles 18:2	p 58
1 Chronicles 16:34	p 82	2 Chronicles 18:3-4	p 58
1 Chronicles 16:35	p 83	2 Chronicles 18:7	p 59
1 Chronicles 16:36	p 83	2 Chronicles 18:10	p 60
1 Chronicles 16:43	p 87	2 Chronicles 18:14	p 60
1 Chronicles 17	pp 23	2 Chronicles 18:15	p 60
1 Chronicles 17:1	p 27	2 Chronicles 18:21	p 60
1 Chronicles 17:2	p 27	2 Chronicles 18:23-24	p 60
1 Chronicles 17:4	p 27	2 Chronicles 18:27	p 60
1 Chronicles 17:16	p 28	2 Chronicles 19:2-3	p 63
1 Chronicles 17:16-27	p 28	2 Chronicles 20:1-30	p 63
1 Chronicles 17:17-20	p 29	2 Chronicles 20:35-37	p 63
1 Chronicles 17:21-22	p 29	2 Chronicles 29	p 101
1 Chronicles 17:23	p 29	2 Chronicles 29:3	p 102
1 Chronicles 17:24-27	p 24	2 Chronicles 29:4-5	p 102
2 Chronicles 16:7	p 60	2 Chronicles 29:6	p 104
2 Chronicles 17	p 55	2 Chronicles 29:7	p 104
2 Chronicles 17:1	p 57	2 Chronicles 29:8-9	p 105
2 Chronicles 17:2	p 55	2 Chronicles 30	p 101
2 Chronicles 17:3	p 55	2 Chronicles 31	p 101
2 Chronicles 17:5	p 56	2 Chronicles 31:21	p 108
2 Chronicles 17:6	p 56	2 Chronicles 32	p 101
2 Chronicles 17:7-9	p 57	2 Chronicles 32:22-31	p 101

2 Chronicles 32:23	p 107	Nehemiah 8:12	p 16
2 Chronicles 32:24-25	p 107	Nehemiah 8:13	pp 18 & 19
2 Chronicles 33	p 101	Nehemiah 8:14-18	p 19
2 Chronicles 33:1-2	p 101	Nehemiah 8:18	p 19
2 Chronicles 33:2	p 108	Nehemiah 9	pp 13, 18, 19 & 21
Nehemiah 2:18	pp 14 & 20	Nehemiah 9:1-3	p 19
Nehemiah 6	p 14	Nehemiah 9:27-31	p 21
Nehemiah 7	p 14	Nehemiah 9:38	p 20
Nehemiah 7:5	p 14	Nehemiah 10	pp 13 & 18
Nehemiah 7:73	p 14	Nehemiah 10:1-39	p 20
Nehemiah 8	p 13	Nehemiah 11	p 18
Nehemiah 8:1	p 15	Nehemiah 12	p 18
Nehemiah 8:5	pp 15 & 18	**Zechariah** 9:9	p 114
Nehemiah 8:7	p 18		
Nehemiah 8:8	pp 15 & 18		
Nehemiah 8:9	pp 15 & 16		
Nehemiah 8:10	p 16		

NEW TESTAMENT

Matthew 1	p 114	Ephesians 6:14	p 97
Matthew 6:9	p 29	**Philippians** 2:10	p 114
Mark 8:36	p 102	**Colossians** 3:23	p 53
Luke 3	p 114	**1 Thessalonians** 1:9	p 56
Luke 18:1-8	p 40	1 Thessalonians 5:17	p 25
John 9:25	p 17	**2 Timothy** 2:22	p 47
Acts 2:29-31	p 113	**James** 1:19	p 30
Romans 8:29	p 72	James 5:19	p 106
Romans 14:11	p 114	**1 John** 3:2	p 72
1 Corinthians 10:12	p 63	1 John 1:7-9	p 17
Galatians 6:1	p 106	**Revelation** 19:11-16	p 114
Ephesians 6:4	p 108		

Published by:

Growth Advantage Communication, LLC

3867 James Hill Circle

Hoover, Alabama 35226

growthadvantage@gmail.com

Made in the USA
Lexington, KY
30 April 2018